NEW ENGLAND'S
GENERAL STORES

Exploring an American Classic

TED REINSTEIN
AND ANNE-MARIE DORNING

Globe
Pequot

GUILFORD, CONNECTICUT

Globe
Pequot

An imprint of Rowman & Littlefield

Distributed by NATIONAL BOOK NETWORK

Copyright © 2017 Ted Reinstein

Photo on page i of Shrewsbury Co-op at Pierce's Store by Art Donahue Photography

British Library Cataloguing in Publication Information Available

Library of Congress Cataloging-in-Publication Data available

ISBN (paperback) 978-1-4930-2879-5

ISBN (e-book) 978-1-4930-2880-1

♾™ The paper used in this publication meets the minimum requirements of American National Standard for Information Sciences—Permanence of Paper for Printed Library Materials, ANSI/NISO Z39.48-1992.

Printed in the United States

For Anne-Marie, Kyra, and Daisy.
With love and appreciation always.

Contents

ONE OF A KIND

THE NEW BREED

"The big towns are getting bigger and the villages smaller. The hamlet store, whether grocery, general, hardware, clothing, cannot compete with the supermarket and the chain organization. Our treasured and nostalgic picture of the village general store, the cracker-barrel store where an informed yeomanry gather to express opinions and formulate the national character, is very rapidly disappearing."

— John Steinbeck, *Travels with Charley* (1962)

The Death, and Life, of the General Store

In the nineteenth century, all Americans knew what a cracker barrel was. Many in rural areas might have lingered around one daily. Today, it's one of those just vaguely-familiar-sounding terms. The Oxford Dictionary defines "cracker barrel" as a *"reference to the barrels of soda crackers once found in country stores, around which informal discussions would take place between customers."*

Definitions aside, for most Americans today, "cracker barrel" simply conjures the ubiquitous and eponymous chain of restaurant/gift shops that carry the name. Ever been to a Cracker Barrel Old Country Store? (If you've been on any major highway in America, you've likely seen its signs). There's a "front porch" of an entrance, replete with rocking chairs and often an actual wooden barrel or two topped with a checkerboard. Customers enter and exit through a waiting area that's actually a gift shop (clever) that offers country-type, "homey" items (apparel, branded food products, etc.). The restaurant's menu features mostly comfort food items such as meatloaf, chicken pot-pie, and "Grandpa's Country Fried Breakfast." The décor is all rustic wood, warm lamplight, and splashes of red and white gingham, all designed to create the sense and atmosphere of an old country store (or country something). In reality, of course, a Cracker Barrel Old Country Store is neither old nor a country store, nor is there a cracker barrel around which you'll find folks gathered and engaged in discussions, formal or informal.

Nonetheless, the chain's creators were on to something when they founded it in 1969. People really like the *idea* of an old country store. Even if it exists in name only, even if it's an ersatz version tucked between an outlet mall, a busy highway, and a string of gas stations. In fact, the appeal of the *idea* becomes even stronger as the reality—actual, surviving country stores—becomes increasingly rare.

"The reality of most places in America today is that it's a suburban experience," observes Cabot Orton of the Vermont Country Store in Weston, Vermont. "They don't have little village greens, they don't have town meetings or volunteer fire departments—or old-time country stores. They have Walmart and Costco. But the idea of an old-time country store is still charming and still so evocative for people."

Sure, in part, it's about nostalgia for a simpler, more innocent time. In part, it's about a longing for authenticity. After all, we live in a world of imitations and replicas. You can pose before the "Eiffel Tower" in Las Vegas, order a burger in a "vintage" 1950s-era diner built in the 2000s, and chase "African elephant poachers" at a Florida theme park. Today, for a place or product to be branded not by marketers, but by over two hundred years of real, living history inspires a powerful sense of credibility and connection with our collective past. Such is the feeling that original, authentic, and enduring general stores elicit today. But however historic, these are not museums. They live, seemingly as endangered species. Habitats that once were supportive become more challenging all the time. The numbers of the old stores dwindle, the remaining ones seem like rarities.

Most historians consider the "golden age" of country/general stores to be the mid-nineteenth century through the early twentieth. In general, income was rising, travel was growing, and trade around the world was expanding, putting products that were once exotic and inaccessible on the shelves of even small-town stores. Of course, that required a storekeeper who was industrious and inventive, which the best ones were.

"The country store owner, in addition to everyday necessities, also brought things from all over the world to small-town America where people weren't able to source imported goods or little indulgences," says Orton. "And so a store owner might find tea from Ceylon, silk from China, he would track down perfumes and hard soaps from France, and bring those things together in a mix that was edited and assorted for the people in the community."

The general store owners of New England had an advantage as well. The region developed early, first as colonies, then as the first states of the new nation. Roads, ports, and eventually railroads developed earlier, also. And because the six states of New England are all within reasonable travel distance to the coast and major maritime cities such as Portland and Boston, getting goods from a variety of sources was easier. For all of this, it is no surprise then that general stores flourished first and most plentifully in New England and no surprise that some of the nation's oldest ones still survive there.

The stores typically developed in tandem with a town center and were usually located where roads and routes intersected. They were invariably solid, often two-story, wooden buildings with little adornment. Form followed function, and the function was to cram as many goods and products into a ground-floor main room as possible. There would be a wooden counter, often with barrels (yes, some filled with soda crackers, others might contain pickles or molasses) in front of it, as well as sacks of flour or grains. There would be walls of wide, floor-to-ceiling shelves, some filled with rolls of fabric, others with other household and practical items (such as pots and pans), canned, and dry goods, coffee, and teas. Various tools and even farm implements might be arranged along the front porch and elsewhere inside, where wooden bins or massive wooden drawers could be sorted through for nails and smaller hardware. To one side of the room, often toward the back, would be a wall lined with inset mailbox slots. (The store-keeper was often also the town's postmaster.) And somewhere in the center of the main room would invariably sit a large, cast-iron, sometimes pot-bellied, stove, whose iron door could be heard groaning open and clanging shut again throughout the day as regular customers would feel free to feed another log into the fire. New England winters are cold, and those same regulars would likely linger for a spell, perhaps reaching into the barrel for a cracker or two while discussing the news around the farm, the town, the nation, or the world.

Cabot Orton's grandfather, Vrest Orton, wrote about his childhood memories of his own dad's general store in North Calais, Vermont, around 1900:

> "Most of the men came in the evenings to wait for the horse-drawn stage that brought the mail from Montpelier, 13 miles away. The store was warm and cozy. It smelled of harness, coffee, smoky kerosene lamps, tobacco and sugar maple burning in the big stove."

There were wars, there was peace, America boomed. Small towns became bigger ones. Even the smallest New England towns, once off the beaten path, became but white-steepled satellites of the huge interstates that now ringed them, however many miles away. People had cars, and people could drive a short distance from their small town to a larger supermarket. There were choices. Options expanded as towns seemed to shrink. The little country store they passed to and from other places now seemed quaint and inadequate. Over time, more stores closed. By the 1980s, even those that remained found themselves squeezed more than ever by the advent of the big box national chain stores, the sprawling, commercial goliaths on the edge of towns that seemed to surround and swallow small towns' main streets—and their small stores—whole.

Whole histories, whole traditions, whole ways of life gone.

Who has time?

But a funny thing happened as the big stores got bigger and the number of surviving general stores grew steadily smaller. And it's a big box store–sized irony, too, because the very forces that threatened to eliminate the general store ultimately helped to save it.

Growth, development, and sprawl had their downsides, too. By the last half of the twentieth century in America, what had become big and convenient and comfortable had also become less appealing in some ways, too impersonal. You might pop into the same place for the same coffee at the same time every day—minutes from your house—yet remain a perpetual stranger. For some, across cities and suburbs—and despite good jobs, nice houses, and quality schools—"desirable communities" often seemed peculiarly lacking something most desirable—community. Increasingly, many neighborhoods seemed to exist in name only; neighbors rarely knew each other. In the seventies, eighties, and nineties, many small towns around New England saw an influx of newcomers. Often from metropolitan and suburban New York and Boston, people transplanted to places such as Barnard and Pittsfield in Vermont, Hope and Whitefield in Maine, and Harrisville and South Acworth in New Hampshire. For many, it was about a career change, leaving "the rat race," and a lifestyle that had become too hectic and harried. For some, it was about finding a place that seemed healthier in which to raise families. For others, it was simply about recapturing a certain quality of life that still seemed possible in small-town New England, where it had never entirely left. Where small-town greens still framed the sacred and the secular—a church, a library, a general store—and where, in each one, they still took the time and the interest to remember your name; to ask about your children, your trip to Florida, your aging mom; and to say, "Hey, we missed you at the pancake breakfast Saturday—everything okay?"

You don't get that at the Safeway near the subdivision. But you do at the South Acworth Village Store, for example. And at a dozen or more others like it.

In many of these small New England towns, what longtime residents already knew, and what transplants soon discovered, was that the vanishing sense of genuine community still held there. And often, it was most vividly exemplified at the general store. It was a place that offered what was lacking elsewhere and filled a need that went far beyond groceries or gas.

In the 1980s, celebrated author and American urban sociologist Ray Oldenburg coined the term "third places." He observed that most people spend much of their lives going from home to work and back again but long for a separate, different, "third place." In a piece entitled "Our Vanishing Third Places," Oldenburg wrote, "What suburbia cries for are the means for people to gather easily, inexpensively, regularly, and pleasurably— a 'place on the corner.'"

These "third places" could be local libraries, cafes, barber shops, beauty salons, taverns, or a post office. Or a country store.

What's in a Name?

The terms *country store* and *general store* are often used interchangeably by the stores themselves. There are some store owners who not only have a preference for one or the other, but maintain there is a difference between the two terms. Perhaps there is, but it's not one that seems significant. Just the same, and for whatever reasons, in general, we prefer . . . (wait for it) . . . "general" store.

"People really long to be connected to a community," says Scott Cole, owner of the Monterey General Store in Monterey, Massachusetts, "even if they're busy or move around, and I think these stores can represent that for many people."

Wherever these stores exist, they are, above all, local, they are a gathering place, they are welcoming, and they know your name there.

"It's these places that really make a community a community," says Paul Bruhn, executive director of the Preservation Trust of Vermont. "And without them, without a place where you connect with a community, we are all just subdivisions."

The stores profiled in this book (with a few exceptions) are very much that "third place" for their communities. It is a huge part of why many stores hang on and why many of those communities refuse to let them go, even if it means saving the store by buying it and owning it collectively. The truth is, long before the term was coined, many of these old stores had constituted a "third place." In that sense, even for some of the centuries-old stores that follow, the real story is not so much how *they* have changed over time, but how we have. And how the humble general store, far from being a relic of an earlier age, is needed more than ever in this one.

A Note on Metrics

This book is not a comprehensive listing of New England's general stores, nor is that its premise. There are many wonderful, longtime, even beloved general stores that, alas, are not profiled here. There is no slight involved, only considerations of space. What we sought was a variety of stores across six states with interesting histories and stories. The resulting panorama is more impressionistic than photographic. That said, we attempted to narrow our search to stores that have been in business for at least a century, have occupied essentially the same building/footprint (always as a general store) since their beginnings, and still represent an enduring business as well as a genuine community gathering place. Were there some exceptions? Yes. Some stores have been included that have morphed into something today that is different from what they represented a hundred or two hundred years ago. These few stores are truly "one of a kind."

THE OLDEST

(IT'S COMPLICATED)

Only about a third of all new retail businesses in America survive for ten years or more.

For family-run businesses, 70 percent never make it past the first generation. The century club? Only 3 percent of family businesses extend successfully to four or five generations. Clearly, it's not easy, whether you're a new restaurant or a rug-cleaner. Or a general store.

Interestingly, though, many of New England's general stores—and nearly all those profiled in this book—have reached the century mark and then some. So many, in fact, that it is now a popular parlor game between such stores to argue over who, in fact, is the oldest of them all. At one time, though, way back in the day, there was no real argument. It was easy to state with certainty which general store was America's oldest.

Oh, for the simpler times of 2012.

In August of that year, Gray's General Store in the village of Adamsville, Rhode Island, finally bit the dust and closed after 224 years.

It had been a good run. Indeed, few American institutions of any kind can claim to have lasted that long. The nation itself has been in business only sixteen years longer.

The key to Gray's longstanding "oldest" title was its *continuous, uninterrupted* run. There are other general stores that go back well more than a century but have closed then reopened. And, even though they have occupied the same physical footprint throughout,

they cannot make the claim of oldest, which would require *staying* open. That takes fortitude. It takes sometimes a succession of owners over many decades who hang in and hang on, who embrace the new while not entirely forsaking the old. It takes generations of individual neighbors and customers who are devoted and loyal. And, collectively, it takes a community that simply cannot—and will not—see itself without its general store.

Are there many such stores left?

Are there many fingers on your right hand?

Truthfully, with Gray's gone, there are now a mere handful of general stores that meet that lofty criteria or even come reasonably close. And, as we'll see, even among the major candidates, there is often some degree of gray area between them. Alas, it truly was more black and white when there was Gray's.

The Old Country Store & Museum

(MOULTONBOROUGH, NH)

Established 1781

On a windy and crisp but sunny October afternoon, I am in the town of Moultonborough, New Hampshire, on the far northern shore of the Granite State's (and New England's) largest lake. Foliage of red, yellow, and orange speckles and dots the hills that rise up and surround the shimmering, blue expanse of Winnipesaukee. Through the brilliant, blue sky to the east, one can faintly discern the dusting of first snow on the summit of New England's tallest, Mount Washington.

In fact, this scene's sense of superlatives would seem to extend to the building in front of me, too—arguably New England's (and for that matter, America's) oldest general store.

It has stood on this same spot for 234 years. It has seen couriers on horseback stop at its door, relating news of General George Washington's election as the new nation's first president. Throngs outside digested the tragic news of Lincoln's assassination, and in the 1940s, young GIs making their way home from WWII popped in here for a Coke (on the house). Through the decades, the Moultonborough store on the side of Whittier Highway at the "top o' Winnipesaukee" has been a steadfast and enduring witness to history. Including its own.

It was built in 1781 from a barn frame and purchased by a fur trader.

"The original room, which is the one behind us," clerk Jonathan Hayden tells me, "is the only one actually original to the store; the rest of it, like this, the post office, all of them were additions from that point."

There is no question the store is old. Very old. The owners have records dating back to 1781. If you're doing the math at home, that would make this store eleven years older than Gray's was at the time of that store's permanent closing. So yes, there is a case to be made here in Moultonborough. And they make it.

"As far as we know, it's the oldest store in the United States," Hayden tells me as we stand next to the venerable, old, white pickle crock. Hayden is married to a Holden,

owners of the store since 1972. (Yes, a wee bit confusing, what with the Haydens and the Holdens, and their respective holdings.)

"We've been told we are one of the oldest surviving businesses in the United States," Hayden explains. "I think we've been bankrupt twice, had at least ten different owners, but it's been in the same family now for thirty-five years."

Some things don't change. From the low ceilings and some of the more or less original, worn woodwork, the store has the unmistakable feel of age and history. But some things do change. Like the basic nature of the store itself. Once this store—like all similar ones in New England—was a neighborhood gathering spot where locals went for virtually all their basics, their mail, or news of the world. Or, perhaps all of the above, topped off with a cup of hot coffee on a cold winter morning with a neighbor or two. But today, that has changed, forcing store owners to think of new ideas to stay in business.

"You name it, we've tried it," Hayden says, rubbing his chin and taking a long view out the front windows toward the darkening lake in the distance.

"There was the store the way it was, there's been ice cream, we had a restaurant here, all those things have gone by the wayside to turn it over to a gift store for some people, and for other people, hard-to-find hardware items or unique gifts."

True, traipsing up and down the narrow, cluttered aisles and disappearing into different nooks and corners of the store brings all sorts of fun surprises. There are whole shelves of authentic duck decoys, dolls, and decorative hardware of all kinds. And who knew there was such a colorful variety of Elmer Fudd–type earmuff hats or that you could still buy a genuine *slingshot* (rock for ammo not included)?

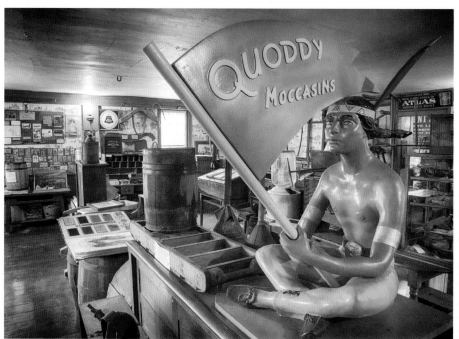

"Yeah, just a good, old-fashioned, simple maple slingshot with a rubber and leather catcher on it," marvels Hayden. "We go through twelve dozen a year."

A tour bus pulls up outside. I mention to Hayden that more customers are about to enter the store in the next few minutes than might have come by in an entire day at one time.

"True," he smiles, nodding. "For many people, it's become a destination, where it used to be, 'Hey, let's stop in there' as they drove by. Now they physically come, and plan on it."

Hayden excuses himself to help a customer whose question ("Got any licorice?") he cannot resist. There is certainly more candy here today to tempt kids of all ages than there ever was in the past. Licorice is a popular item, particularly because many returning customers are aware of the enormous (and sometimes exotic) selection.

"Oh, we have licorice like you wouldn't believe," Hayden says with a wave of his hand at the jars behind him. "What are you after?"

I wander off and climb the stairs to the museum. There is local flavor, for sure, though little to do with the store itself—a section of old wooden pipe; a vintage, yellowed Sears catalog; a pair of century-old skis with leather binding straps. On the ground floor, there is an authentic and flawlessly preserved Concord Coach, the stage coach that originated in Concord, New Hampshire, and was made famous by Wells Fargo.

Before leaving, I chat again briefly with Hayden, who finishes up a sale with a friendly older visitor from Ohio on a leaf-peeping tour. The visitor is delighted with the antique cash register, still in use on the counter. A sign on the wall above it reads "Shipping Happens."

I ask Hayden what a visitor from a century ago would find most familiar about the store today.

"Maybe the pickle crock," he says, gesturing toward the container.

I lift the lid and inhale the tangy aroma.

"Pickles are still a huge staple item for us," Hayden says. "You wouldn't think in Moultonborough, New Hampshire, that we'd sell 13,000 a year."

I would, actually. With help from Ohio and all those tour buses from everywhere else. There's nothing wrong with that. You change what you need to in order to survive and keep what works. The proof is in the pickles.

About That Name . . .

South central New Hampshire—Hillsborough County—is aptly named. It's an area of gently rolling hills that roll ever higher as the terrain rises northward to become the White Mountains. Those hills were once dotted with farms, dairy mostly. Then the railroads came, and by the late nineteenth-century, so did summer tourists from Boston and New York, lured by those cool, verdant hills. Today the farms are mostly gone, and so are the grand, sprawling, wooden hotels where the summer visitors stayed. But as you drive through the region, you can still see some homes, an occasional farm, and assorted other buildings all from an earlier era. The Mont Vernon General Store, sitting and selling on the same spot since 1840, is one of those living relics.

The town of Mont Vernon (its 2010 population was just over 2,000) lies a bit north of neighboring Amherst, New Hampshire, from which it separated in 1803. And no, that's not a typo about the missing "u" in "Mont." Depending on who you ask, there are various explanations: Some say it was a clerical error, others that it was a deliberate effort to distinguish the town from the many other Mount Vernons named after George Washington's home. Still others maintain it was a nod to the large French-Canadian population that was drawn to the area a century or more ago. Either way, the case of the missing "u" seems to point to a peculiar issue the town seems to have with names in general.

In 2013, Dan Bellemore, a friendly fellow nearing fifty, bought the store, but it wasn't called Mont

Photo by Ted Reinstein

Vernon General Store at the time, having gone through a few name changes. One previous owner had given it the dubious name of "Blood and Temple," which referred to two nearby streets but sounded more like a pop-up store for pagans and devil-worshippers. More inexplicably, another previous owner changed the store's name to, of all things, "Fishbones." Bellemore wisely changed the name yet again. After all, he had dreamed of owning a genuine general store; he wasn't going to finally buy one and call it "Fishbones."

Earlier, in 2012, after drawing some negative national attention, the town changed the name of a local pond from "Jew Pond" to "Carleton Pond." While that name change came about only after a contentious (104-33) town meeting vote, it's likely that, had a vote been taken, a name change involving the local general store would have sailed through with even less dissent.

"Yeah, I am sure glad the name was changed back to Mont Vernon General Store!" laughs Bellemore.

Having grown up in nearby Bedford, New Hampshire, Bellemore remembers coming to the store as a kid. When it went up for sale, he thought he could tap his unique business skill set to make a store work. "I always wanted a store," he smiles, standing behind his gleaming, wooden counter on a quiet Sunday morning. "I was on the road for twenty-five years in business, and I always was drawn to stop in small, local general stores—I saw the good, the bad, and the ugly!"

Photo by Ted Reinstein

Bellemore is energetic and creative and is determined to keep the locals happy while offering some new and innovative wrinkles to attract others.

"Most people come in and are surprised," he says. "It's like a little step back in time, but with a twist—we do the windows like Macy's, do wine tastings. On the other hand, I had a guy come in one time, buy some carrots, and take 'em out front to feed his horse. People were surprised by that, too."

After all the new frills and twists, Bellemore swears by the importance of offering good food. The customer who's just grabbed his Sunday paper with a fresh breakfast sandwich seems to agree.

"If you want to make money with your store, you have to do good food," Bellemore says after wishing the man a good day and watching him leave. "But I wouldn't recommend someone at fifty-two doing this—you have to love it or don't do it."

Bellemore clearly loves it. And all the wonderfully unpredictable things that come with it. Like the couple who had met at the store and then dropped by for their fiftieth wedding anniversary. They were going to grab sandwiches. Nothing doing, Bellemore told them. He had them sit on the porch, where he ran speakers out to play Big Band tunes while personally serving them lunch.

"My favorite moment so far," Bellemore says, and smiles.

Wayside Country Store

(MARLBOROUGH, MA)

Established in 1790

Sudbury, Massachusetts, is about 23 miles west of Boston. It's a quiet, leafy, and relatively affluent suburban town of about 18,000. It was incorporated in 1639, and like that of most other New England towns named after one in Olde England, Sudbury's history is literally layered in centuries. The town boasts some of America's first, first-responders. In the early morning hours of April 19, 1775, 250 Sudbury militiamen answered Paul Revere's alarm and marched to neighboring Concord's North Bridge to confront British troops. (Sudbury can also boast America's most prized zip code: 01776.)

One of Sudbury's most legendary and enduring landmarks is the famous Wayside Inn.

Its license as an inn was granted in 1716, almost sixty years before the first shots were fired in Concord and Lexington. The poet Henry Wadsworth Longfellow later popularized the inn in his "Tales of a Wayside Inn," published in 1863. A different Henry—Henry Ford (1863–1947)—bought the inn and thousands of acres surrounding it in 1923, hoping to create a sprawling history-themed village and museum there. Ford never realized that particular vision, but he did add several elements (such as the famous grist mill) that still draw visitors today. Ford, the last private owner of the Wayside Inn, ensured the property would be preserved by a public trust when he sold it in 1945.

In 1929, as part of his original plan to create a Colonial village in Sudbury, Ford moved the town's venerable general store. Built in 1790, the store conducted its business in the town's small but historic center for 150 years. But Ford liked the idea of the historic store being closer to his historic inn, so a team of oxen hauled it several miles down the road (today's Route 20) to the edge of Hager Pond in what is now Marlborough, where it continued doing an uninterrupted business. Or so today's present owners thought.

Bob and Debbie Eager bought the store in 2006 from Debbie's parents, Anthony and Joan Scerra. The Eagers promoted the store as one of, if not the, oldest continuously operated general store in America. And why not? For over 220 years, the Wayside

Country Store had long nipped at the heels of New Hampshire's Moultonborough store, which itself had been around for barely a decade more than that. The two vied for the title of "Oldest and Continuous" until 2010, when, in the course of some researching, the Eagers were forced to confront some jarring new information about their storied store's past: Its operation had not been continuous and uninterrupted after all. And it had only taken one man, his odd quirks, and his hair-trigger temper to temporarily shut down his own store.

There was more to Henry Ford than the car company that still bears his name. He was, no question, a brilliant and fabulously successful American industrialist. Through mass production, he made the automobile affordable, and he helped pioneer the assembly line that turned out his product. But did you know that Ford also had an apparently intense if irrational aversion to canned food? (Not to be confused with his similarly intense and irrational aversion to Jews.) No, you didn't know that. Who knew that? Not one particular poor, unsuspecting store clerk, that's for sure.

"Ford came by to visit his store one day in the 1930s," Debbie Eager tells me as we stand inside that same store on an early October day in 2010. "He came in and noticed a can of Campbell's tomato soup under the counter, which was the clerk's lunch that day."

Not for long it wasn't.

"I guess Ford assumed that his 'no canned food' rule was strictly followed, and he apparently was incensed on finding the can," Eager explains. "He took the keys, shuffled everybody out the door, locked it, and threw the keys in the pond out back."

So much for lunch.

With the keys on the bottom of the pond, the store closed, and the owner off on a tin can–induced hissy fit, the Wayside's heretofore uninterrupted run of continuous operation was, well, interrupted. In fact, the store was closed for approximately seven years before reopening. After decades of believing that their store, like Moultonborough, had never closed, this was most distressing news for the Eagers.

"So, Debbie," I ask, "but for a can of Campbell's soup, you would still be competing for the title of 'oldest continuously operating country store' in America."

"That's right."

"That has to hurt."

"It does, it does."

The store today functions much like Moultonborough, though—less of a community gathering place than a tourist stop. Not that locals have no reason to stop by, especially with kids in tow. The Wayside Country Store's candy section is the largest you will likely ever see. And from the original wooden floors to the old stove to the back door where an irate Henry Ford flung the keys into the pond, much of the store's long history is still there. Just don't ask if they carry canned soup.

Jericho Center Country Store

(JERICHO CENTER, VT)

Established in 1807

Jericho, Vermont, is one of a number of New England towns with a biblical name. Others include Hebron, Connecticut; Canaan, New Hampshire; and Galilee, Rhode Island. Needless to say, that's where the similarity with the ancient Middle Eastern city ends. No palms, date trees, or shifting sands in northern Vermont. (Though, much like sand dunes, snow drifts do reshape in the wind.) Jericho is located about 20 miles east of Burlington, the state's largest city, and in the shadow of some of the Green Mountain's tallest peaks.

Jericho Center has a quintessentially New England quality to it. There's a village green, surrounded by a variety of proud, old, white frame buildings in which townspeople have

Photo by Art Donahue Photography

Photo by Art Donahue Photograph

gathered for different purposes for centuries—churches, a library, and a town hall in which one can easily imagine a New England town meeting scene right out of a Norman Rockwell painting. At one corner, across the street, is another town landmark in which locals have also gathered for centuries: the Jericho Center Country Store.

"It's almost like it keeps watch over the green," says General Manager Jon St. Amour. "And really, it has, for over 200 years." St. Amour has a good perspective on the store. He grew up with it, and around it, and today co-owns it with his parents, Doug and Linda.

"The store has been here for so long, everyone around here knows it and has their own stories and history with it, from your mom, to your grandmother and great-grandmother," said St. Amour. "I mean, it's the only show in Jericho Center!"

Not that progress and change and modernity haven't licked all around the land just miles from that pretty, little changeless town green. Big box stores now beckon from off the interstate. But that contrast—and competition—are part of what makes this store's long-running story unique.

It opened in 1807 as more of a trading post. Its first proprietor was a man named Pliny Blackman, who seems more like someone out of Grizzly Adams than a store owner. Blackman would raft north on Lake Champlain, making his way via the St. Lawrence River to Montreal, where he'd procure goods to bring back to his store. There, he'd sell and barter his new goods, his customers often trading eggs and produce for hardware and farm supplies.

Other owners made their own mark over the ensuing centuries, most notably the Jordan brothers, who owned the store for nearly forty years beginning around 1900. Around the same period, the store burned but was rebuilt in much the same size and shape as it

Photo by Art Donahue Photography

appears today. In the 1960s, Gerry and Lil Desso took over the store and are credited with making the store into what it is perceived as today—the heart and soul of the center of Jericho.

"We grew up in nearby Richmond," remembers St. Amour. "My dad worked in the store as a teenager. The store was beloved by us."

And then, it was for sale. St. Amour and his younger brother were out of school and working, but living at their parents' place.

"It had just popped up on the market, and we just kind of huddled and said, 'Hey, it would be a neat thing,'" St. Amour recalls. "Actually, my parents were like, 'Let's get the kids out of the house.' We went to the bank and got a loan, and bada bing, here we are."

First there was the dirty work. St. Amour describes the store when his family took over as, "beat up, ramshackle, falling part—it needed a ton of work." It got it. Over six months, the store was basically gutted, cleaned up, repainted, and reinvented somewhat. Not that the process was free from worry.

"We knew how special this place was," he says. "People still loved it even though it was run-down. It was a true Vermont general store, but people weren't buying their hardware here anymore, the big boxes were already in Williston. We knew we had to rein-vent the place."

So hardware, the staple of an old-time general store, was dispensed with. Food was the new focus. Good, quality, locally sourced ingredients for good sandwiches. It was new and different and served a need. It caught on fast. But it wasn't easy bringing everyone in town along on the reinvention.

"The old-timers who'd been coming in for decades came in and looked at us and were skeptical," St. Amour concedes. "But we were upfront and honest—we told them we have to do this, that this store will not survive, and we have to change."

And it's worked. The business has grown steadily over the past fifteen years. The staff, full and part-time, has expanded to twenty; there's a full grill now and pizza.

"It's still only about 1,800 square feet of retail space, so it's not huge," shrugs St. Amour. "Sometimes there are lines snaking through the shelves, so it's quirky, but that's also part of the charm."

It's real and authentic and still a living part of this town.

"There are a hundred people who come in every day and get their mail and pick up the milk," St. Amour says. "We see our customers every day and we get to know them as friends. It's not a big box store."

Sure, the craft beer and Vermont gifts sections have expanded, while hardware has vanished and groceries have shrunk. But for Jon St. Amour and his family, the changes and reinvention have always been about ensuring that the beloved Jericho Country Store survives.

"I'm thirty-eight, I started at twenty-three, almost half my life," he says. "I have four kids and my wife grew up two houses down from here and we would come into the store. Now our kids are growing up in the store, too. My oldest is twelve; she likes to come in after school and count money, and she'll come in and do big meals with me for the army base down the road. My other daughter is in fifth grade and will go around and dust shelves. And my mom—well, this was her vision. She always loved this store, and she kind of looked at this big, dusty, crazy cluttered place and she had this image. And all these years later, we have kind of achieved what she thought it could be."

Haunted Hardware

Rhode Island may be a small state (okay, the smallest), but it does have the biggest official state name: "State of Rhode Island and Providence Plantations." But even more, it's a charmingly pugnacious little state that punches way above its weight. (Texas's tired old "Don't Mess with..." slogan? Please. They'd make quick work of your cowboy hat in Cranston.) Its early detractors (including legendary Puritan sourpuss Cotton Mather) derisively referred to the colony as "Rogues Island." It was, in fact, an early haven for outsiders of all kinds, starting with its founding in 1636 by Roger Williams, who himself had been banished from the Massachusetts Bay Colony for his more tolerant religious views.

Clearly, there is a lot of colorful history in Rhode Island. No big surprise, then, that for a long time it boasted two of the oldest general stores in the nation. Until it finally closed in 2012, Gray's in Little Compton, Rhode Island, was the oldest general store in America. Today, in the nearby village of Chepachet, Brown & Hopkins Country Store makes the case that it is now America's oldest, continuously operating general store in the same location. Could be. (As we've seen, these kinds of distinctions can be distinctly inexact—and hotly debated.)

What's fact: The building that still houses Brown & Hopkins was built in 1799. By 1809 (the year Abraham Lincoln was born), it was in use as a general store. It was purchased in 1921 by James L. Brown and William W. Hopkins. They had a good run; the store was next sold over forty years later in 1964. But the Brown & Hopkins name has been kept ever since, through a succession of owners. The store's current owner, Elizabeth Yuill of Foster, Rhode Island, purchased it in 2004.

"There's been over seventeen owners in the last two hundred-plus years," Yuill says. "So each owner has left a little piece of history behind, and we call that our 'Wall of Honor,' the things that are not for sale, just for show."

Those "little pieces of history"—a jumble of relics and artifacts—are artfully arranged behind the counter and include a massive vintage cash register, century-old scales, and an earlier owner's carefully handwritten store ledger. Visiting on a bright but brisk March late afternoon, I am welcomed by a huge, classic potbelly stove that, alas, offers no warmth. ("Retired but still admired," as Yuill puts it.) In truth, much of what this store once was when that old stove still blazed has been retired, too. Today Brown & Hopkins is an upscale gift shop specializing in homemade craft items and "fine primitive country wares" as Yuill describes it—reproduction furniture and hardware, period lighting, quilts, fabrics, candles, and curtains. But while the shelves may now hold period paints and gourmet items rather than canned goods and cereal boxes, there is no doubting the genuine feel of age and history here still. It can't be missed, from the wide, pine floor planks that still creak and bend to the original ceiling beams. There's a penny candy corner, and they'll even ring up your little paper bag of treats on that big, vintage register. Inventory may have changed, but physically little else has, making it very easy for a visitor to imagine the store in another, earlier era. In fact, some say that emissaries from that earlier era may sometimes return.

"Oh, yeah," smiles Yuill. "I do think we may have 'visitors' from time to time."

Others are more definitive about that. Teams of paranormal investigators have insisted that recording devices left overnight in the store have picked up various voices, footsteps moving about, and otherwise difficult-to-explain noises on all three floors of the building. (Cameras have not detected actual images.) Yuill does describe her own ghostly experiences—like the time she opened the store in the morning to find some rearranging had apparently been done overnight.

"There was a mannequin on which we had hung a dozen or more silk scarves," says Yuill. "When I came in, I noticed that all of the scarves had been very skillfully knotted together."

But it's all good in Chepachet. The spirits seem very benign, and the possible hauntings only seem to add to the sweeping historical lore of Brown & Hopkins. Besides, one spirit is apparently a neat freak who works off-hours, shows initiative, has a sense of style, and does product arrangement for free. What merchant wouldn't want a ghost like that around?

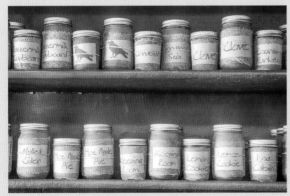 

Photos by Art Donahue Photography

COLEBROOK STORE

BUILT 1812

BUILT 1782

Colebrook Store

(COLEBROOK, CT)

Established in 1792

Colebrook, Connecticut, is next door to the Tunxis State Forest. Which has nothing what-soever to do with general stores, but it's fun to say Tunxis, isn't it?

Actually, Colebrook is also surrounded by the Litchfield County towns of Norfolk, Win-chester, and Barkhamsted. The area sounds more like Olde England than New England. It is only fitting then, it seems, that Colebrook is home to Connecticut's oldest general store.

But wait, it gets better (or older, as the case may be). The Colebrook Store was long considered to have originated in 1812. (It says so right on the vintage sign above the front door.) That's plenty old as it is and had already landed the store on the National Register of Historic Places. But in 2016, original and previously undiscovered records were uncov-ered establishing that the store actually opened twenty years earlier, in 1792. This made the Colebrook Preservation Society (CPS) very happy. (Only when it comes to historic buildings is being twenty years older cause for celebration.)

"We found the store journals two years ago," says Gerry Kassel, curator of the CPS. "It showed both the front and back parts of the store were in operation in 1792. They sold flour and nails."

The store was opened by two brothers, Martin and Soloman Rockwell. The list of suc-ceeding owners over four centuries is, needless to say, long and varied. Alas, by 2007, the store seemed to have reached its shelf life. In fact, the shelves themselves were mostly empty. The owner at the time and the store both seemed to have run out of gas, and the store closed. A run of 215 years of continuous operation was broken. So were a lot of local hearts.

"We are right across the street," says Kassel. "It was hard to look at it when it was closed. It was empty, mind you, but random people would still plant flowers in the flower pots outside. The man next door noticed the flag was all faded and kind of hung up by the pole; and he got a new flag on there. We just didn't want it to look like an abandoned child."

Neighbors cared so much about what had been abandoned in their midst—and lost in their community—that they finally just went ahead and adopted it. In 2013 (for a paltry $85,000), the Preservation Society bought the general store and set about nursing the "abandoned child" back to good health.

"A lot of the problems were the building needing so much work," says Kassel. "The Preservation Society had fund-raisers, they insulated it, they put in new windows, they fixed the foundation, they did everything they could possibly do to make it a safe and livable place. Otherwise, the people who were running it [would be] overwhelmed with just the upkeep."

There were hiccups in finding the right person to operate the store, and it closed again briefly. But on the auspiciously catchy date of 12/13/14, the store reopened once more under the operation of Jodi Marinelli.

"I thought, well, hopefully the date is good luck," laughs Marinelli. "They wanted very much to preserve the building, they wanted the store to come back, and I thought it would be great to be a part of that."

Marinelli had been working at another general store in Riverton, Connecticut, but she was the overwhelming choice of the store's owner, the CPS, to be the new operator. With her fiancé and her two kids, Martinelli moved into the apartment above the store and set to work making it an inviting and appealing hub for the small town once again.

"Jody just clicked," says Marty Neal, a store regular and a member of the Preservation Society. "Look, it's a tiny town; you need someone who can open at six a.m., make a good egg sandwich and coffee, all with a smile. She does that!"

Marinelli does quite a bit more than that. She's turned the store into a legitimate eatery in a way it never was. And she brought back a traditional Colebrook Store favorite: éclairs.

"They had been done for years here; we brought them back," said Marinelli. "They're good; both visitors and summer people will stop in and say, 'Can you ship me some?'"

The busy little kitchen also does homemade soups, chili, sandwiches, and cookies. The cooking is a family affair. Her sister runs things with her ("She's my right-hand man!"), and her dad comes in every Thursday to bake fresh muffins and scones. In addition to her three "adult" employees, she loves to offer work to local kids, who line up to make a few bucks sweeping and mopping the store. It's only two rooms, including the kitchen in the corner of the main one. The smaller room, where the town's post office used to be, now comprises the store's small grocery section. A few small tables and chairs fill out the main room. It's cozy, with lots of waving, lots of lingering to say hi over the tables.

"It isn't just a community gathering place—it's the *only* real community gathering place," says Greg Hoffman, a genial, semiretired contractor who's lived in Colebrook for thirty-five years and is in the store every day for coffee. "I knew Jodi from her first store in Riverton; we are so lucky she's here. This store came so close to closing for good; people would drive by and wonder, 'Where are we going to go?'"

As if on cue, a woman stops by to say hi to Hoffman. When I look back, another friend has joined them.

"You might start with two people at the table, and then chairs are getting pulled from various places and you might wind up with nine people at the table," laughs Gerry Kassel. "Remember *Cheers*? That's what it's like in Colebrook—everyone looks up at the door and you almost always know who is coming in."

"The whole town comes in here and they mix well," says Marty Neal's husband, Chip. "I should know—I'm in here every Saturday with the guys."

"Or Tuesday or Thursday," interjects his wife, laughing. "But all kinds of people really are in here all the time, from the guy who plows the snow, to the New York lawyer up for the weekend—and they might just have breakfast together, too!"

The casualness belies some thoughtful touches. Martinelli has begun live music events at the store once a month. By the coffee area in the middle of the room, a large checker board is laid out on a big, old, wooden barrel. Next to it sits a small box holding both checkers and chess pieces.

"I love looking out at that when I'm busy cooking over there," smiles Martinelli. "So often you'll see some young boy or girl invite an older person to play checkers—and they always do."

The checker board barrel is only one element that illustrates just how old this store and this building are. More than most equally old general stores I've visited, there is an uncommon sense of authentic age and history here. The elements of modernity around the faded,

dark wooden edges—a display cooler, kitchen appliances, sleek coffee carafes—don't seem to dissipate the overwhelming feeling of how genuinely *old* this place is. Which means that, despite the store being back in business, the building's owner, the Colebrook Preservation Society, has ongoing work to do to further preserve what is a living link to the eighteenth century. The $200,000 in donations and grants has already gone into basic structural upgrades and improvements, including the restoration of the four huge Doric columns on the front exterior. The rehab of the venerable building's exterior continues with siding and roofing work and repair of the old, crumbling chimney. The Society hopes to have the work all done in time for the building's 225th anniversary in 2017.

Meanwhile, Jodi Martinelli continues her own rebuilding, from the inside out, and with each sandwich, and soup, and smile, shoring up faith anew in a beloved gathering place that is thriving and inviting once more.

"I feel so lucky that I've been so accepted here," she says, looking around the quiet store's fading light on a winter afternoon, snow flurries wafting by the front windows. "Because this has been my dream."

It's been a town's, too.

"Of Special Note . . ."

Williamsburg General Store, Williamsburg, MA

Williamsburg, Massachusetts, is nestled in the foothills of the Berkshires. There, on Route 9, in the heart of Williamsburg, is the Williamsburg General Store. The store is more than a hundred years old, which won't come as a surprise to anyone who has ever stepped inside and made the worn, wooden floor creak. There is still a noticeable dip in the original wood floor where the postmaster used to sit.

Heather Majercik, who manages the front part of the busy store, says that when her father, David, bought the store in 1977, it had frankly seen better days. Today, the store is spruced up and thriving with a large gift shop, a popular ice-cream parlor, and a bakery that entices regulars from both ends of the state to stop by and stock up on the store's trademark product—the "Wrapple."

"I always grab some for the kids," says Maureen Huminik, who grew up in nearby Whately but now lives in the Boston area. "This is how I grew up, but we don't have general stores like this in Eastern Massachusetts; there's a little something for everybody here!"

Photos by Ted Reinstein

Legend has it that Heather's mom, Carol Majercik, came up with the idea for the Wrapple more than thirty years ago. It consists of baked apples wrapped in the middle of a pie crust with a dash of cinnamon. (Traditionalists will tell you it's only complete with a splash of vanilla icing on top.) There are "dry" periods during the year when the Wrapple is unavailable, usually due to the fact that all of the store's apples come from a single local grower in neighboring Cummington. If the farm is out of apples, the store is out of Wrapples.

Regulars and first-time visitors alike comb the store's narrow little aisles on the lookout for the odd and unusual.

"To me, it's a place to find things you just won't see at box stores," says Alexis Dow, a regular on a late-summer Sunday morning browse. "I always see something I didn't see last time."

If you stop by the back bakery counter for a Wrapple, make sure to say hi to Evelyn Mulcahy. Now eighty-four, she's worked at the store for twenty years.

"It's such a wonderful store," says Mulcahy, "and the people who run it are so lovely, too."

I was lucky enough to get my Wrapple fresh out of the oven. I'd have more to report on what else Evelyn might have said, but she was adamant.

"Eat that while it's warm!"

So I did.

Photo by Ted Reinstein

The Brewster Store

(BREWSTER, MA)

Established in 1852

It should come as no surprise that one of America's oldest general stores is on Cape Cod.

In 1620, the *Mayflower* landed first at what is today the town of Provincetown, on the Cape's outer tip. History is as commonplace on the Cape as sand and surf. In fact, the Pilgrims' own history is echoed in the town of Brewster, named as it is for Elder William Brewster, who was the first religious leader at Plymouth Colony. Brewster sits at the "elbow" of Cape Cod's bent "arm." European settlers were building homes and farming

Photo by Ted Reinstein

there by 1656, but it wasn't incorporated as a Massachusetts town until 1803. In 1852, the Universalist Society built a two-story church building for itself. Let's just say that, where religion apparently didn't flourish, commerce did. Over the next century and a half, what had started as a church evolved into something more secular: a general store. One that, today, seems in some real way like the true beating heart of Brewster.

Considering its long history, what's most remarkable about the Brewster Store is that it has had less than six owners. Equally significant is that while each one made some changes or added services, the store itself retained its same basic look and physical profile for 150 years. Each owner seems to have had a respect for the history they inherited.

One owner, Donald Doane, had perhaps a little *too* much love of history. In the early 1960s, he briefly turned the store into a museum. Thankfully, the museum didn't take, and he reopened it again as a store. At one time the local post office was located in the store. Windows were enlarged, a porch was added. But over time, as one looks at photos through the decades, the front façade has changed remarkably little. The store today looks much like it did a hundred years ago.

In the 1970s, then-new owners Bob and Faith Dibble set the store on the path it most resembles today. Longtime summer residents of the town, they changed the store's name to the Brewster Store. The Dibbles already owned a country store in Pennsylvania and had a love for disappearing, outdated, or simply hard-to-find household items, from odd kitchen gadgets to replacement parts for lanterns, to vintage hand tools, some of whose specific function could often confound a contemporary shopper. In the late 1980s, the Dibbles sold the store to George and Missy Boyd, who enthusiastically shared their predecessors' love of all things old, practical, and hard to find.

From the outside, with its oversized, multipaned windows, wide stone stairs, and antique wooden benches, the Brewster Store simply looks like what most people would see in their mind's eye on hearing the words "general store." On entering, it's hard to know where to look first. There's so much piled around you can see only a fraction on first glance. A tidy corner to the immediate right has newspapers stacked for local subscribers; on the opposite wall are bins of "penny" candy (the cheapest costs twenty-five times that). A wooden staircase goes up to the second floor, where the Boyds exhibit their own love of local and national history. But the rest of the first floor is all business. Locals pop

Photo by Ted Reinstein

in for a coffee and a donut, some fresh popcorn, or ice cream in summer. In winter, a pot-bellied stove warms the main floor. (You'll want to look for the cracker barrel.) The aisles are filled with mostly very practical merchandise. (Although an entire section is laden with old-fashioned glass lamp chimneys, as if the Victorian era had never really ended. In this store, one can partly pretend it hasn't.)

"This is a general store" George Boyd is fond of saying. "And if someone comes in looking for something, we want to have it."

It's no surprise that the Brewster Store, especially in summer, attracts a huge number of tourists. It sits on Route 6A, also known as the Old King's Highway, which winds along Cape Cod Bay through other historic Cape towns such as Sandwich, Barnstable, Yarmouth, Dennis, and Orleans. In this sense, the store is not tucked away in a small town square where locals on a coffee run might be surprised to see many "outsiders." On the other hand, the store long predates Cape Cod's more modern persona as a tourist mecca. It caters to more than locals now, though a visit in midwinter will give a visitor more of a sense of what things felt like a century ago. But it's still there, a part of history.

And part of a small club that only gets smaller as history moves on.

TRIED & TRUE

Did you grow up near a corner store? In many urban and suburban neighborhoods, they come as close as you can get to a rural area's general store. The merchandise doesn't tend to be nearly as general, and you won't find hardware, clothing, or a post office. You will generally find a variety of necessities, though, from milk and bread, to aspirin and razor blades (not to mention non-necessities, like newspapers, cigarettes, beer, and wine).

Often called variety stores, some in the Boston area—don't ask me why—were called "spas." (Patronizing one was not the equivalent of the modern-day "spa treatment.") The corner store I grew up near was about six blocks from my Boston-area home. An older, constantly bickering couple ran it. I was always awed by the proprietor's uncanny ability to quickly total up my mound of candy and gum spread on the counter before him merely by eyeing it, then unerringly take my money and make change if necessary—all the while carrying on a pitched argument with his wife, who was often on the other side of the small store. You can't teach that skill. (And I can't think of little Braff's Variety Store without recalling it.) But for a generation, for certain things, a whole neighborhood depended on that little store. It was good to know it was there, it was close, and it was familiar, like an extension of your own home (sometimes complete with the arguing).

It was nearly always open, too. It was there before you were born, and it was there when you grew up, perhaps moved away. It was "tried and true." In more rural areas, where there is less choice and more distance between stores, such stores do—and must—stock more general merchandise. They are similarly depended upon, and often their presence is measured in multiple generations. That's all true of the following general stores. And there can be no argument about it.

Granville Country Store

(GRANVILLE, MA)

Established in 1851

Even Massachusetts residents who know their way around the state can be forgiven if they can't quite place the town of Granville.

It just sounds a lot like some other places.

Granville sits just over 100 miles southwest of Boston in the low hills of Hampden County and just east of the higher Berkshire hills of the state's western border. But Granby, *Massachusetts,* is situated only some 50 miles northeast. And to make matters even more confusing, Granby, *Connecticut,* lies just over the border, a scant 14 miles to the southeast. That's a lot of same-sounding names to keep straight.

Maybe this will help: Of the three relatively neighboring "Gran" towns, only Granville is named for John Carteret, the second Earl Granville and seventh Seigneur of Sark KG PC. (Try putting that on a business card.) Clear enough, right?

Photo by Ted Reinstein

What's actually much more interesting than Granville's name is its location. It abuts the town of Southwick, which is most famous for being the Massachusetts town whose peculiar southern border forms a sudden dip, or "jog," into Connecticut. Look at a map and follow the Massachusetts border west toward New York. The boundary line with Connecticut is perfectly arrow-straight until Southwick. There, sure enough, and for no apparent topographical reason, the border seems to sag of its own weight and suddenly plunge a mile or so down into Connecticut before righting itself, rising up again, and soldiering on, straight ahead, to the New York line.

Weird.

There is, however embarrassing, a perfectly (or rather, imperfect) human explanation for this dip. The infamous "Southwick Jog" is the result of a seventeenth-century surveying error. One that has never been corrected. The surveyors (henceforth known in Connecticut as the "drunken mathematicians"), who'd been tasked with creating the Massachusetts/Connecticut border, simply miscalculated as they set out from just south of Boston. Because they were fearful of crossing through the then-dense woods of south central Massachusetts, they opted instead for a far more complicated but seemingly safer surveying method. They took a reading at the known southern border with Connecticut, then jumped on a ship out of Boston, sailed around Cape Cod, south through Long Island Sound, took a left at Essex, sailed north up the Connecticut River, where they disembarked closer again to the (still to be formalized) Massachusetts border.

The (clearly not) intrepid surveyors' plan was to use their last reading from south of Boston and then extrapolate from their new position to the west to account for the distance in between, then continue on to the New York border. Brilliant, right? I mean, what could go wrong?

"Well, what happened was, their readings were off," explains Pat Odiorne of the Southwick Historical Society as she looks over a map clearly showing just what a botched job the surveyors did.

"So it was a mistake, right?" I asked.

"Yes, it was a mistake," she confirmed.

And an apparently permanent one, too, for while Connecticut has long chafed about it, short of making a trip before the US Supreme Court, there's nothing to be done to rectify it. But it sure makes for a lot of fun cross-border name-calling still today.

Granville, meanwhile, merely sits next door to the Southwick follies. Its borders are beyond reproach and untouched by controversy. In fact, there's a lot that feels untouched in Granville. It's a quiet, wooded, rural town, just over forty square miles in area in which just over 1,500 people live. It has a lovely, classic New England town green (flag pole in the center) with a proud, nineteenth-century stone library off to one side. On another side sits a low, white, one-story wood building. "J.M. Gibbons Sons, 1851–1935" reads the spare, simple signage facing the street and the green.

But then, if you've done business in the same spot for well over 150 years, how much advertising do you really need?

John Murray Gibbons opened his country store in Granville in, yup, 1851. While he sold essentials to his townsfolk and those passing through, Gibbons was most passionate (some would say obsessed) with making cheese. Not just any cheese, either. Gibbons was partial to cheddar cheese that was exceptionally sharp and tangy. "Ripened on the vine," as he put it. It turns out that the deep, dark, stone cellar of Gibbons's store provided the perfect conditions, or "vine," as it were, to age just such cheese. And the rest is . . . well, you know.

Over time, Gibbons outsourced his secret cheese recipe to a dairy/cheesemaker but still "aged it up," as he liked to say, in the store's cellar. And through a succession of four more owners over the decades, that's how it remains today. In 2006, mother and daughter Tina Deblois and Tracy Mountain bought the store. Tracy largely runs it now with her husband, John.

On a busy midweek October lunchtime, it's clear the store is Granville's focal point. By the window, a couple of local cops are eating sandwiches. Nearby, a few town highway workers are doing the same. The store consists of one large room. Aside from the half-dozen small tables by the front windows, there are rows of shelves heading back to the rear of the store, on which sit both grocery items and local products from maple syrup to crafts. But the real business end of the store is the left side, where the long wooden counter runs from the little coffee nook all the way down to the little kitchen area in the back. Up above it, like a silent, sepia honor roll, sits a row of old photos of all the store's previous owners.

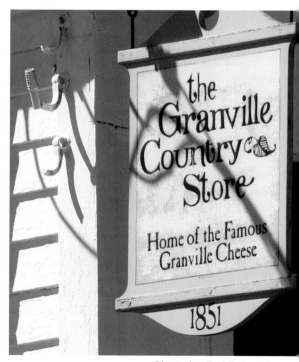

Photo by Ted Reinstein

At the counter below them is their living, breathing, full-color successor—John Mountain. A cheerful, dark-haired thirty-something with a youthful face, he's busily wrapping up a sandwich for a regular customer.

"Yup, hanging on to history here," he says, in between exchanging pleasantries with the man. "We don't change much up here, we just try and keep it the way it is. These stores are now few and far between, and you learn to know all of your customers."

As he turns to leave, Mountain's customer, a middle-aged man in a barn jacket, kids him about having a reporter in the store. ("You ready for your close-up, John?") But the customer is not kidding about what makes him a regular here.

"I guess the best way I can describe it is it's unique," he says, surveying the interior, waving to one of the cops. "It has all the staples, plus some things you wouldn't expect—there's fresh baked goods every day, pies every day, they do their own bread."

He gestures to the small sign above a section of the counter that reads "Cheese."

"Then there's the cheese," he says, taking a dramatic pause as if he is about to swear to something for the public record.

"I've lived in ten states and three countries, and I've lost track of everywhere I've visited. And I have never tasted better cheddar cheese than what they make here."

Duly recorded.

It's a sentiment I'd heard from others in Granville even before my first visit to the store. And it's one I'm inclined to swear to as well after tasting the cheese for myself.

"The extra sharps age for four or five years," Mountain tells me as he expertly works a single wire through a huge cheddar wheel. "Yup, just a good, old-fashioned cheese wire. It may take a little longer, but I know it's gonna be done right. I can cut three blocks in an hour."

The store sells about 55,000 pounds of cheese a year. They ship regularly to individual customers around the country and wholesale to a western Massachusetts supermarket chain. Mountain has dabbled in some different flavors, but plain cheddar (sharp, medium sharp, and extra) is clearly the specialty.

The front door's bells jangle. A hearty wave, and Mountain goes to grab a block of cheese for pickup.

"Thanks, enjoy!" he says with a big smile.

The bells jangle again as the customer exits; Mountain tidies up the cheese counter.

"I meet so many different people," he says, looking out toward the town green. "I know them by name. Sometimes it's not like coming to work, you know? You put a lot of hours in, but it's where you want to be."

Mountain had his eye on the store even before he owned it.

"I saw it back in the nineties, I lived up here, and I said to the owner, if you ever want to sell it, please let me know first. And he did. He found me, and I put it together."

I ask him to what extent it's a gathering place for the town.

"All day," he smiles. "The old folk come in, in the morning, they have their coffee, they talk the town gossip a little bit, I kind of do my thing, they help themselves to the coffee, they'll leave the money on the counter. Saturday mornings are packed with them—Saturday's the big meeting!"

There is a quality that is unique to small towns and a small town's general store. Folks who come in are rarely in a hurry and, on entering, almost unfailingly look about to see if they recognize a friendly face. I share that thought with John Mountain. He smiles, agrees, and nods in the direction of the front windows.

"It's close-knit, everybody watches out for everybody. Not a lot of change, we try to keep it country, keep it nice."

It's quieter in the store. Mountain is cutting up some cheese to ship. He pushes a small slab of sharp cheddar toward me on the counter.

"Try that with a nice little Prosecco wine, some crackers, you're home."

"That is some good sharp cheddar," I say. "Nicely done."

"Thank you. That keeps us on the map, right there."

That would be Granville, on your map. Not to be confused with anywhere else. Nor is its signature cheese to be missed.

X Marks the Spot

When Abraham Lincoln was two years into his presidency, Fiske's General Store opened for business in a sturdy, simple, two-story wood building at the intersection of Washington and Central Streets in Holliston, Massachusetts. For 150 years, it has been a landmark and fixture in this former rural farming town. Now a busy Boston bedroom community of just over 13,000, Holliston claims Fiske's is its heart. That's particularly appropriate because at the center of this town's heart sits a love story. And any customer can see where it all began merely by walking in the front door.

The store was first opened by James Fiske, whose portrait still hangs in the store. Early on, Fiske's General Store sold clothing, groceries, even railroad tickets out of the tiny storefront. The store changed hands several times over the years, eventually settling a century or so later in the hands of a father-and-son duo, John and Louis Paltrineri, which is where the love story begins.

It was a busy and all-hands-on-deck period of time for John and his dad in those first few hectic months of owning the business. Louis spent most of his time on the ordering, while his youthful and amiable son, John, spent his days behind the counter. Then, in April of 1973, John's life changed forever. A young woman with long, blonde hair walked into the store to pick up some Sunday newspapers for the drugstore down the street where she worked. She drove up to the store in a 1946 Dodge coupe, a flashy car that John couldn't help but notice, along with her smile.

"I told her it was a cool car," smiles Paltrineri.

After the mystery woman left, John spent the day trying to track her car down. He figured it wouldn't be hard to find the flashy vintage coupe in the small town where most locals drove sensible late-model Fords and Chevys. He found the car at last in a parking lot a mile away and left a note on the front windshield wiper: "I would like to get to know you and your car better."

Smooth.

Photo by Ted Reinstein

John crossed his fingers. It worked. Carol called a day or two later. And the rest is, as they say, Fiske's General Store history.

The pair did connect, and although Carol went off to college and they spent some time apart, she eventually found her way back to Holliston—to Fiske's, and to John. The couple married and had a son. And these days, if you look carefully at the green carpet just in front of the counter, you'll find an X marking the spot where John first saw Carol that day back in 1973.

"I don't know how many years ago I put the X on the floor across from the register right near the front door, maybe thirty years now," says John. "When the X gets a little worn, some little boy or girl will come in and tell me that the X is wearing away, and then I give them a big marker or some tape and they draw it in again."

The store still sits in the middle of town. You will still find John—and sometimes Carol—behind the counter. Fiske's sells board games, cards, candy, town spirit wear, and all the latest toys. Balloons hang from the ceiling and seem to be everywhere. When the phone rings these days, it's often someone with a suggestion for a new toy to carry or a local Girl Scout troop hoping Fiske's might donate to a fund-raiser. John almost always says yes. Every September, local teachers post their supply lists, and Fiske's makes up "to go" bags full of supplies for each grade. For local Realtors, the store is one of the first stops they suggest new families make when they move to town.

"I have seen the community come together in so many ways," says John. "It's wonderful how people connect."

As that X on the floor attests, he should know.

The Warren Store

(WARREN, VT)

Established in 1839

Warren and Waitsfield, Vermont, are two neighboring ski towns, each fabled for its own legendary mountain. Warren is home to Sugarbush Resort; Waitsfield is home to Mad River Glen, which boasts some of the toughest skiing in the East. Mad River's slogan is "Ski It If You Can." It might just as easily apply to living year-round in this northern reach of Vermont's Green Mountains.

Photo by Phil Bobrow

"The school buses stop here, even the UPS trucks stop here when they can't navigate the icy roads—all the stuff's dropped off here and the people come down."

Where they come down to is the Warren Store. Just like they have since 1839. Not that owner Jack Garvin goes back quite that far.

"I started in 1980," laughs Garvin, a tall, good-natured, middle-aged guy with premature white hair. "I joke that I came in for a cup of coffee and never left."

Most days he really doesn't leave. Especially on long winter ones when it's dark by five o'clock and the sun doesn't warm anything up anyway.

"If you own or manage a country store, it's a 24/7 proposition and it's difficult to leave. That's how it is; there are challenges every day, some are good, some not so good."

For sure, northern Vermont winters are no picnic. Which makes a place like the Warren Store that much more invaluable to folks for miles around. It's been that way for a long, long time. The Warren Store began life as a simple stagecoach stop halfway between Boston and Montreal. Since then, it's housed a hotel, the town's library, and the post office. Later it became a hardware store, and for more than the last fifty years, it has been what it is today, a buzzing and inviting place that pretty much defines the essence of what it means to be a country or general store. Quite simply, it is the heart and soul of Warren.

"Everybody knows it; it's the focal point of the whole Mad River Valley, really," says regular Ron Jacobs. "Once you come here, you know the Warren Store, and you keep coming back. It hasn't changed since it opened!"

That's partly true. Okay, maybe mostly. If you look at photos of the outside of the store in the 1940s, it looks strikingly unchanged. For that matter, the inside looks pretty similar, too. On a recent bright but chilly early March morning, the big, old, cast-iron woodstove in the main room's center was crackling away, much the way it's always been here, making it easy to imagine big, ol' Nashes and Studebakers pulling up outside rather than SUVs and Subarus festooned with "Ski Vermont" stickers and roof boxes. On this day, if one looked carefully, one would see that the venerable woodstove was adorned with a topical and contemporary dead giveaway to its age: a new, hand-lettered nameplate above it. As part of a "name the stove" contest, the hands-down favorite turned out to be "BURN-IE," a fond and apt nod to the state's junior US Senator and, at-the-time (2016), Democratic presidential candidate, Bernie Sanders.

"He comes in once or twice a year," adds Garvin. "'Course, he's been a bit busy lately."

For others in the Warren area, it's more common to come in once or twice a day. And why not? Aside from the coffee wall across from "Burnie," there's breakfast and lunch. The huge and creative sandwiches here are legendary. (How big are they? I have often noted how many miles I have driven before finishing one; 30 miles or so is a given.) There are shelves of basic groceries ("provisions" on the sign, thank you), but also lots of Vermont specialty foods. Like cheese. Cheese is to Vermont what peaches are to Georgia. And then there is beer. Over the past decade or so, Vermont has become something of a mecca for locally brewed craft beer. ("The Beermuda Triangle," it's been dubbed.) Early each Thursday morning, "Thirst-Day," the store sells small batches of the best local brews, including what is, for some craft beer connoisseurs, America's alcoholic ambrosia of the moment, Vermont's own, Heady Topper. In the predawn, cars with out-of-state plates begin pulling up outside the store.

Photo by Phil Bobrow

"We woke up at 4 a.m. and drove up here from Boston," says one happy thirty-something as he loads a crate of beer into the trunk of his car. "We just made it by 8 to get in line, and we were happy to do it."

One of the regulars, a member of the store's vaunted Breakfast Club, watches with bemusement as he sips his coffee.

"I just chuckle when I see the line of people, and the MA plates carrying cases of beer."

"It all comes back to blaming Massachusetts, doesn't it?" I laugh.

"You got to blame somebody!"

Tough room with the Breakfast Club. They commandeer a big round table by the stove every morning. Nothing will deter them. And nothing escapes their notice.

"We're open 364 days a year and they are here every morning," laughs Garvin. "They sit here and solve the world's problems. Or at least they think they are."

It's all in good fun. And it's all part of how the Warren Store has continued to survive and even flourish. Trying new things, keeping traditional stuff, too.

"You can't be everything to everybody," says Garvin. "But you aspire to that, sure. Look, it's Vermont. We realize people who come up here don't like a whole lot of change, so we're mindful of keeping that old feel. We have a lot of people who are invested in this place—they'll say, 'You shouldn't do that,' or 'You should have this.' They're part of the family here and I love it!"

Garvin may not say it, but he and everyone who lives year-round in Vermont (even the die-hard ski bums) love it just a wee bit more when the warmer months finally come. Which, contrary to popular rumor, does happen. (The calendar year in Vermont has been described as "eight months of cold, four months of pretty poor sledding.") In summer, there is a deck just outside the store where folks can sit and sip their coffee or eat their sandwiches overlooking a pretty brook flowing alongside. The warmer months also bring more tourists to the valley and the store. Sure, there's more eye-rolling among regulars waiting to pay for their lunch while Stu and Shelly from Syosset try to decide between the T-shirts or the cheese sampler. But somehow they all coexist. Somehow.

"Yes, we get the tourists," nods Garvin. "But we also get a lot of the second-home owners from around here, and they know the store, and they all come in, and it's kind of a social hub, kind of a 'meet you at the Warren Store' kind of thing."

Popular meeting spot and postcard-pretty scenes aside, Garvin is a hardnosed realist when it comes to running a general store. He ought to be. He's also current head of the Vermont Alliance of Country Stores. He knows the landscape. And general stores often seem as endangered a species as the vanishing Vermont dairy barn.

"Yes, we are endangered, sad to say," observes Garvin. "On an average, there are two that go down every year; it's really difficult."

Like grizzled Vermont Yankees facing another winter, general store owners do what they need to, to survive. And if they're lucky, they do. If they're especially lucky, they get to sit with the Breakfast Club on a clear, cold March morning, drink hot coffee, and have their faith in humanity (or at least the future of general stores) restored.

"This place just has a great, older feeling," says Jacobs, looking about the room with an expansive wave of his hand. "With the old wood stove over here, and you come in, and it's nice and it's warm, and comfortable, and you know people, it just . . ."

No need to finish, or say more. The other guys nod silently as they sip.

This will do.

Your Money's Worth or Your Money Back

F.H. Gillingham & Sons is a true family business. In fact, it might be more accurately called "F.H. Gillingham & Sons, wives, daughters, in-laws, and great-grandchildren." Because, in various capacities, generations of Gillinghams have continued to be part of the legacy of this store, which was first opened in Woodstock, Vermont, in 1886.

The store's first proprietors were Frank Henry and his wife, Ada. Clearly a man with a flair for marketing, F.H. came up with the slogan "Your Money's Worth or Your Money Back," and the family has used it ever since. Early on, Gillingham's delivered groceries in town by wheelbarrow on what amounted to little more than a dirt path. As a true general store, it had a symbiotic relationship with local farmers: The store sold needed supplies to the local farmers who, in turn, supplied the store with fresh produce and dairy goods. For many patrons, bartering for what they needed was as common as paying cash. Many of those early customer records still exist in the daily ledger books preserved by the Gillinghams as part of the store's history.

Today, Elm Street (the original winding dirt path, replete with many original elms) leads into the center of busy Woodstock, and the iconic store is part of the town's fabric by now. As central as the store is to the town, it's equally central to its own family.

"Since 1886, there has been a family member in charge the entire time," says Jireh Billings, who now co-owns the store with his brother. But there was a time in the 1950s when the family came close to losing it.

"My grandfather died, and my uncle Bill had to leave his job to come and run the store, but he died in 1962. Only my father was around then, and he was a lawyer and a judge, so my mother had to step in and run it," says Billings. And she did.

The world around the store has changed dramatically since it first opened, but many of the old touches inside remain. The wide pine floors are still there, as are the nail bins, the rope-operated Otis elevator, and the National Cash Register dating to the nineteenth century.

But time marches on as it always does. Woodstock is a popular town for second-home owners from Boston and New York, and it's fall foliage and winter ski industries bring a steady stream of tourists and visitors year-round to the postcard-pretty town, which, on some days, can look more like a Hollywood set designer's version of Vermont. (Woodstock's population of 3,000 swells to double that in the summer and fall.)

Jireh Billing's mom recognized that the store would need to keep up. In the 1970s, she decided to stock upscale kitchen wares. The idea for an extensive wine cellar followed shortly afterward. The old

Photo by Ted Reinstein

standbys like nails and hammers lost ground to more sought-after items like Darn Tuff socks, Carhartt, and Under Armour clothing. (Although you can still find a shelf full of glue and batteries.) The cash register, while still on display, was replaced by a modern scanner, the nail bins now hold handmade wooden toys, and the elevator exists now more for a bit of retro decoration than anything else. Of course, like any self-respecting Vermont general store of any size or type, there's a wide range of genuine maple syrup products to be found.

Jireh Billings and his brother recognize that they have been very fortunate. These days, when so many other general stores are going out of business, F.H. Gillingham's is flourishing.

"We are very lucky to be in Woodstock because of the way it developed. Every store is really a reflection of the town it is in. When you think about the institutions in Woodstock, you think of Gillingham's."

Calef's

(BARRINGTON, NH)

Established in 1869

Mary Chesley Calef was a visionary businesswoman, an entrepreneur ahead of her time, a teacher, and a native of outspoken New Hampshire. She might have gone a long way in politics as well as business. Too bad, as a woman, she wasn't allowed to vote.

It was 1869, and Ulysses S. Grant was president. Calef decided to open a store. Not that she had spare capital or investors to do it. She mortgaged her family's farm, added her own meager savings, and opened a small country store in the front two rooms of her simple, wood-frame house in Barrington, New Hampshire. It's still there and still in business, but it's long outgrown the two front rooms.

Photo by Ted Reinstein

"I love history, and I love a compelling story," says store owner Greg Bolton. A native of nearby Candia, New Hampshire, Bolton had been in the food and catering industry for years before buying Calef's in 2013. "When the store went up for sale, it was something I was interested in maintaining."

When Bolton bought the store, the first thing he heard from locals and regulars was that he better make sure to maintain Joel Sherburne on staff. It's hard to fully describe Joel, as he is simply known. But it's also hard to describe Calef's without him. Part loyal and (very) longtime employee, part heart and soul of the store, Joel is also quite simply the closest thing to a bona fide general store celebrity in the otherwise humble and understated low hill country of Strafford County.

How long has Joel been working at Calef's? Well, Grant wasn't president. But another famous former general (Eisenhower) was.

"We had everything in those days—clothes, shoes, hardware—everything!" Joel says, sitting at a round table in the store's main front room, a busy summer Saturday mix of locals and tourists passing all around him. He gestures at the folks passing by. "You knew everyone who came in, knew their name. You don't do that today."

But legions of Calef's customers know Joel's name.

"Honestly," Bolton says, holding up his open palm as if taking an oath, "people come in and the first thing they say is, 'Is Joel still working here? I was last in about twenty years ago and I still remember him.'"

He's hard to miss. Tall, lean, piercing blue eyes beneath a shock of white hair topping off a white-apron over his sweater vest. Joel began working at Calef's in 1956 when the Calef brothers were still running the store. He was still in high school when he was hired to stock shelves.

"Didn't last too long—I was too valuable!" He smiles wryly. "It was the focal point of the town back then—if you wanted to know what was going on in town, you came to Calef's."

That's changed a bit. But then, so has the town. Not as rural as it once was, today it's partly a bedroom community for some of the larger towns and cities that sprawl in southern New Hampshire nearer to the Massachusetts border. What hasn't changed is that Joel still works every day, though he's cut back to four hours (5 a.m. to 9 a.m.). He's also the official ambassador of the neighboring Rochester Fair for ten days every fall. With his distinctively New England voice, he's done radio commercials for both the fair and the store.

Locals dart in early for coffee and something to eat in the car. Others pop in at lunchtime for the variety of sandwiches from the deli counter. Sitting square at the intersection of New Hampshire Routes 9 and 125, the store's hard to miss, and tourists and passersby find it hard not to stop, however briefly.

"A lot of stores are not as lucky as we are with our geography and location," Bolton observes. "We offer locals the things they need every day, like the deli, but we also offer things that are unique for the tourists—a true old experience."

There's the venerable pickle barrel; it's the real deal and one lift of the lid (providing you like pickles) is an aromatic pleasure. But one of Calef's true links with its long and colorful past is its cheese. While the cheese is made for them in Vermont and New York state, Calef's does take pride in their aging process and the unusual sharpness of its trademark "Snappy Old Cheddar." Joel traces its roots to about 1890, when Mary Calef's son, Austin, was running the store.

"A couple of fellows came in and asked him for the sharpest cheese he had," explains Joel. "Austin went down into the cellar and found a couple of pieces of cheddar that had been lost behind the other aging wheels. He offered them to the men who said, 'It's so sharp, makes a man sit up and take notice.'" Folks are clearly still taking notice; the store sells nearly 20,000 pounds of cheese a year.

The porch of Calef's is much the same as it was when Joel stocked items on it as a teenager, all the better to turn someone's head and come into the store. The wood floor still creaks as it did under the boots of Calef kids past. An ancient woodstove sits there, once the sole source of heat in the room. But there is no denying the careful blend that Bolton has tried to create between the old and the new.

He is still, after all (and as any good general store owner should tell you), running a business, not a museum.

"I certainly consider myself a steward of the history here," he says. "But there's always a balance between the history and running a business. Sometimes there's pushback, we try to balance it, but yeah, it's balancing the tourist stuff and the local stuff, and it's hard sometimes, it is."

Bolton is no doubt heartened by the reality that the store does well. He employs twenty full- and part-time people, and, as of 2016, sales at the store were up 25 percent over the previous four years. Maybe Bolton really has found that elusive sweet spot between holding on to history and the locals and blending in some new wrinkles for the outsiders. As a living link between the two, Joel Sherburne is just happy to be part of it all. Still.

"What I love about working here is the atmosphere; people walk in, they light up right away, like something from their childhood. It's a pleasure to come to work every day—not everyone can say that!"

Of Special Note . . .

Alley's General Store/West Tisbury, MA

In summer, on the front porch of Alley's, you'll find an unusually large selection of beach chairs, beach toys, and boogie boards. (And a very popular swing.) But, as any successful store owner knows, you cater to the community you're in, and Alley's is on the summer playground island of Martha's Vineyard. In fact, the store is the island's oldest-operating retail business. As such, you'd think that Alley's would have every advantage, but it's actually had to overcome some distinct disadvantages.

Ask any general store owner how he remains in business, chances are his answer will include some variation on the fact that he sells prepared food, beer, and wine. These items are the bread and butter of almost any general store that still has with an "Open" sign on the door. But Alley's can't sell any of these items. West Tisbury is a dry town, which means no liquor sales. And because of a long-standing agreement with a neighboring deli shop, Alley's doesn't sell sandwiches. This puts Alley's in a bit of a pickle, if you will. What's a general store manager to do? Well, to hear store manager Rhonda Backus tell it—try to sell just about everything and anything else.

"I have everyday things, nice things, and quirkiness all under one roof," says Backus. "I hope it's fun for people."

It sure is a fun inventory: brie and Barbie dolls, hammers and nails, foil and fish hooks, measuring cups and milk, T-shirts and tea. Customers still pick up their mail every day inside the store, kids choose candy from the candy counter, and the morning rush in summer is a tangle of residents and visitors all converging for coffee, newspapers, and conversation. It's an island tradition, and a genuine community gathering spot. And it continues to be a prized place for celebrity sightings. After all, even famous actors, musicians, and journalists crave the simple pleasure of a coffee or an ice cream at some point in their starry and super-exciting celebrity day.

The store first opened its doors in 1858 (when there were way fewer celebrities). A man named Albion Alley bought the store in 1946 and changed the name to Albion Alley and Co. By 1964, it was known simply as Alley's. The store became a vital part of the Martha's Vineyard community because supplies can only come in by flight or ferry. Still, the community is a small one, and after a quick succession of owners couldn't make a go of it, the Martha's Vineyard Preservation Trust bought the building and the business in 1993, undoubtedly saving this beloved island institution.

These days, many would also credit the dedication and creativity of Rhonda Backus. Alley's is thriving. In summer, there's now a farm stand outside, local musicians often play a set or two on the back porch, and on the famous front porch, well, the morning coffee crowd remains a daily ritual as dependable as the sunset just down the road at Menemsha, just more caffeinated.

IT TAKES A VILLAGE

Mad River Glen is a small but legendary ski area in Fayston, Vermont. In the age of sprawling, splashy ski resorts, Mad River Glen remains a unique and iconoclastic outlier, kind of like the state's junior US Senator Bernie Sanders. In fact, Mad River Glen is the kind of ski area at which Sanders would feel very comfortable. In 1995, the area's owner decided to sell it to a group of skiers who had formed a cooperative in order to maintain local control of the beloved mountain and to prevent an outside owner/developer from coming in and making dramatic changes. It's worked out well, shares are still publicly sold, and shareholders attend "town hall" meetings to discuss issues (also very Vermont).

Across New England, there are also a small number of general stores that survive today because of the same spirit that saved Mad River Glen. These are stores that were similarly local, beloved, and whose history had become woven into communities that were unwilling to lose them. Members of those communities banded together, formed boards and associations, raised money, volunteered time and effort, and either bought the store themselves or found ways to partner with another entity also committed to preserving the store. It takes a pretty special store to inspire that kind of devotion. It takes a pretty special town, too.

South Acworth Village Store

(SOUTH ACWORTH, NH)

Established in 1865

"Like a home away from home, that's how I describe it," says local resident Linda LaCasse as we stand on the front porch of the South Acworth Village Store. "It's the feeling you get when you walk into the store, that 'Ah, I'm home.' I hear the kitchen noise, some rattling around, someone is cooking some sandwiches, some soup, there's comforting noises in the background—people love that. I think that's why people love to be here."

For LaCasse, it was something of love at first sight.

"My husband and I were looking for some land to build our house, and we kept driving through this town, and we kept stopping at this store. And people were friendly, and the

Photo by Art Donahue Photography

place smelled great, and they had fresh bread and local goods, and we just fell in love with it, and I knew I wanted to be a part of it."

LaCasse and her husband did build their house here, and today she is very much a part of the store. But that's modern history. On this day in the fall of 2015, a vintage red and white Chevy pickup pulls in. Its owner, a tall older fellow with longish white hair under a ball cap gets out with a big old dog. They make their way slowly to the store's front door, which opens with a familiar jangle of bells. Linda LaCasse watches them and smiles; the scene makes her think of the longer history of the proud, old building they've just entered. A history that predates her as well as the guy, his truck, and everyone else in town.

"A hundred and fifty years—that's a long time," she says.

It is.

"You gotta think about what was going on [in] this world 150 years ago, and this store was here."

I do think about it.

In 1865, Union soldiers from the hill country of west central New Hampshire would have begun returning from the just-ended Civil War. Along the Cold River in the little mill village of South Acworth, they would have found a newly established general store. It was named Union Hall, a symbolic nod from some grateful northerners for their side's success in keeping the young nation whole.

In time, the Union would reknit itself, and in the decades to come, the Acworth Village Store would knit itself ever more tightly into the fabric of this hardy hill community. It was a gathering place, a grocery store, a post office, and, aside from the church, a truly shared space that transcended everything else including, unlike the church, religion. (You can talk politics freely in a general store, but religion is more iffy—the exact reverse is true in a house of worship.)

Black-and-white photographs of the store from the 1920s, '30s, and '40s show not only the changing times themselves (horses give way to automobiles), but the ways in which the physical face of the store changed as well.

There were a few other stores around, but the Brick Store on the hill burned down in 1915 and Grammie Knight's closed in the 1950s. Only the Union Hall kept going.

"They sold nails and gasoline, food and fabric, whatever was needed at the time," says LaCasse.

In truth, the store sold anything and everything mostly to spare local folks the grinding twenty-mile trip over rough roads and hills to larger stores in Keene to the south.

And so it continued, even as the mills that had once dotted the area disappeared and the local population dwindled. The sturdy store survived the Great Depression and two world wars, but the transition to the twenty-first century seemed, alas, finally a bridge too far. In 2001, the store's then-owners, Dick and Nancy Stuart, who'd run the store since 1986, decided they'd had enough. With no immediate buyer, the only option seemed to be to sell things off and close up shop for good.

Not so fast, said South Acworth.

"The townspeople said, 'We can't have that,'" recalls LaCasse. "This is the heart and soul of the town, and the town simply said, no—we've got to find a way to save the store."

So they did. They started a Save the Store campaign and formed the Acworth Community Project. Because really, that's what it was about—saving something that was central to their sense of community. The local historical society, having successfully secured a grant, was able to get a mortgage and buy the building. But, as LaCasse wryly observes, owning a building doesn't run the store that's in it.

"Then it was like, okay, now what? How are we going to run this?"

They formed a board of volunteers. It meets once a month to determine what needs to be done, to solicit feedback from customers about what's working, what's not, and what should be done differently.

"The board sets the vision for the year, what sort of events we want to have, what sort of new things do we want to add, and we really try hard to make it come true," said LaCasse.

Certainly, there's no lack of creative ideas. A few years back, someone suggested they build their own pizza oven out back.

"Done," points out LaCasse proudly.

"We have different events throughout the week, we have Saturday night pizza, and on a monthly basis we try to have big events here—we do a music fest in June, we do farm to table in the fall, we just had a pig roast last weekend to get more people involved, to get more people here."

Whatever it takes.

"A lot of sweat equity, a lot of community involvement," agrees LaCasse.

The store does have a few paid staff, such as Kevin Davey, who manages the store's daily operations.

"I come in at 5:30, and we get the early risers like the town highway crew going—feeding 'em breakfast, making coffee," explains Davey.

It's lunchtime on this day, and Davey and his assistant are busy working the grill behind the counter.

"The people who come in, they keep you going." The white-aproned Davey smiles, spatula in hand. "I do the post office, manage the store, run the register, I cook. . . ."

He waves to a gray-haired woman in a red sweatshirt who is retrieving her mail on the other side of the store.

"We all do whatever it takes."

In South Acworth's case, it truly does take a village. People really do turn out for all the store's special events, but they also drop in regularly throughout the day, grab a coffee, a sandwich, a bowl of soup. The store also pays the local support forward to their surrounding neighbors on a daily basis, diligently selling mostly local products. On this day, I had just come from a visit to Orchard Hill Breadworks in nearby East Alstead, where I sampled what might possibly be the best bread I have ever tasted. And there, on a shelf just below the Acworth Village Store's front counter, I spot fresh loaves of Orchard Hill bread. Nice.

But people have to actually buy that bread—as well as the coffee and the breakfast sandwiches and the pizza and the other products—if a store like this one (or any other) is to survive.

"They support us, and they come here on purpose," says LaCasse. "And people who've been away for a while, like summer residents, will come in and say, 'We're so happy we're back at the store.'"

The store is relatively small but feels comfy in its old, creaky, wooden way. A hand-painted sign by the front door says simply "Hot Food." Just inside, along the front windows, lay a row of old booths using reclaimed church benches. To the sides of the store are mailboxes and shelves of grocery items, as well as local crafts. In the center, the counter

bends around in a sort of half U, where people sit and chat over coffee or a sandwich. The grill is out in the open, all the better for Davey or his help to converse with their customers, all of whom seem eager to talk with each other, too.

"One thing that villages like this and towns like this lack are meeting places," says Ken Grant, a seventy-something board member and long-ago transplant from Ohio.

Grant has been sitting at the counter, engaged in deep conversation, punctuated by loud laughs, with the guy who walked in with the dog.

"I mean, we have our meeting house," he continues as we move outside. "We have the church, but there are very few places where people can go every day or go casually to buy something or to hang out, and the store is about the last place in town where that can happen."

A younger, bearded man with a big dog loping alongside walks by. A nifty-looking SUV now sits next to the vintage Chevy pickup outside the store. There are contrasts here, but the store seems to be the community's common thread.

"There are a lot of people here you wouldn't think would be here," observes LaCasse. "A lot of artists, poets, furniture makers, potters, fiber artists. They come here to be alone but also be part of a community—the store is really the community part."

On this day, noontime has become midafternoon. With lunch over, Davey is cleaning the grill and tidying up the counter. I ask LaCasse what it says about her community that it wasn't willing to let its little store disappear.

"I think people who live here really like the simple life, they like life at its simple basics, and to be able to walk to the neighborhood store to get your basics is what people have done for a very long time. They love that. And it is *the* gathering place. I think that's what's lost a lot in today's world, and it's one of the reasons I came here. I love being part of the community."

We shake hands. By the edge of the porch, a big ol' golden Lab lies contentedly on the faded wood planks warmed by the afternoon sun. LaCasse gestures and laughs as she heads to her car.

"See? Even the dogs love it here."

Shrewsbury Co-op at Pierce's Store

(NORTH SHREWSBURY, VT)

Established in 1865

Where else but in Vermont would you expect to find the Cold River? And in south central Vermont, you'll find the Cold River just a bit north of Shrewsbury. In North Shrewsbury, you'll find a remarkable general store with an equally unusual name: Shrewsbury Co-op at Pierce's Store. Its history is pretty unusual, too.

The simple, white, low-slung, clapboard building at 2658 Northam Road in North Shrewsbury has been a combination home and general store since the mid-1800s.

Photo by Art Donahue Photography

Sometime around the end of World War I, the Pierce family purchased the store and lived in the attached house. And Pierces continued to do that for seventy-five years. Marjorie Pierce was the last child of the second generation to run the store. In 1992, in her nineties, she felt she'd just plain had enough and decided she would close the store. Which she did. No one in North Shrewsbury could begrudge a woman for wanting a wee bit of retirement after all those years. But they sure wished the store didn't have to retire along with her.

"Marjorie really began to feel that the community missed her store," says Paul Bruhn, executive director of the Preservation Trust of Vermont (PTV). "She realized the store was the one place in town where people really connected with each other. And it was gone. I think she really felt that."

No, Pierce wasn't coaxed out of retirement. But she did approach Bruhn and the PTV with an offer: She would give them the building, plus some additional money, providing they would find a way to reopen the store.

The Preservation Trust's mission is to help communities save and use historic places and to support local preservation efforts. It does this through a wide range of assistance programs and technical guidance, as well as helping to provide funding and secure outside grants. It does *not* save historic places by actually taking them over. Piffle. Marjorie Pierce had other ideas.

"She really twisted Paul's arm," says Sally Deinzer, president of the Shrewsbury Co-op at Pierce's Store. "She said, 'Please do this—I will give it to you, and then I want you to find someone to run it and reopen the store.'"

Bruhn agreed, and the PTV reluctantly became the store's owner. (It remains only one of two properties the PTV owns outright.) They then embarked on a concerted mission to find someone else to actually operate it. They posted ads in the *New York Times* and *Boston Globe* and got responses. Nothing seemed like the right fit. Instead, the answer ended up being much closer to home.

"When I first moved to town—it was after the store had closed—people would say the sense of community in town had disappeared," recalls Deinzer. "And I would say, 'Are you kidding me? There's a great sense of community! There's a school, a church, a library.' But the longtime residents pointed to their closed store as a huge loss. They really missed being able to go in there and pull up a chair to the woodstove, they missed that the Pierces knew everybody and that there was no place like that now."

So Deinzer and some others asked a simple question: Why can't we reestablish that?

It wasn't easy, it wasn't quick, and it certainly wasn't without some notable bumps in the road. The group decided to form a cooperative and submit a formal proposal suggesting that they lease the store from the Preservation Trust and run it as a co-op.

"They actually laughed at our first proposal," admits Deinzer. "It had to have financials, a detailed business plan. We weren't exactly businesspeople—the only person with retail experience was a woman who had run a bookstore. So there was a lot of learning by the seat of our pants."

But they were committed and determined locals with the best sense of their own community, what they missed, and what they wanted to regain. For their part, the Preservation Trust was properly skeptical but nonetheless loved the idea of a local group taking control; that is, after all, what the PTV is all about. So they had meetings with the prospective Shrewsbury cooperative. It only took one such meeting for Paul Bruhn to realize that this was the way to go.

"We had one community meeting, it was early on in the process, and a couple of neighbors, who lived 100 yards apart, as they were coming to the meeting said to each other, 'Gee, I haven't seen you in months!' And they lived 100 yards apart. That's what happens when you don't have a place like the store where neighbors run into each other. This is why they matter. This is why they are missed when they go away."

The cooperative was given the green light for the lease and set about first doing major fund-raising. Their timing was not opportune. It was May of 2008, the height of the Great Recession. They did broad appeals, targeted appeals, and by September of that year had raised over $60,000 and had also received a matching grant from the Trust.

In shifts of volunteers, they set about cleaning the store, which at that point had been closed for over a decade and was showing its age. The PTV stepped in to update the plumbing and electrics, but the store needed "serious cleaning," as Deinzer puts it. It was decided, however, that the cleaning would not include getting rid of some of the old-time, historic charm of the original store, including its legendary smoke-stained dark ceiling.

"Apparently, it's like a hundred years of creosote and cigar smoke up there," laughs Deinzer. "And they said don't even try to do anything with that—so we didn't. And I think it's one of the most charming things about this."

Freezers were installed, supplies arrived, shelves were carefully stocked, the volunteer board took a deep breath ("a lot of fear and trembling," laughs Deinzer), and on August 25, 2009, after being closed for fifteen years, the new/old Pierce store reopened to customers.

The support was immediate and strong. But exactly two years after opening, the fledgling, newly reopened store was tested anew, this time by Mother Nature.

Photo by Art Donahue Photography

In August of 2011, Hurricane Irene blasted up the East Coast, made a terrifying turn inland, and made a beeline for Vermont, a state that is not used to taking a direct hit from even a weakening hurricane. Up and down the state, damage was massive. Rivers overran their banks; roads collapsed; and centuries-old, iconic covered bridges were swept away like so much spindly driftwood. The town of Shrewsbury was hit hard, but the hardy, low-to-the-ground Pierce store stood. The volunteers went in, hunkered down, and turned on the emergency generator. The lights shone. The sturdy little general store beckoned through the wet, windy darkness.

"We had power, we had working internet and telephones, and that brought everybody out of the woodwork," says Deinzer. "Once their road was open, they traveled here. We became information central."

"Irene hit in just our second full year of operation," remembers Deinzer. "It was just developing, the sense of the store being at an important place. And we were there when people needed us. So many people said, 'Oh, you are such an asset.'"

Today, in good weather and bad, the tidy little store that withstood the storm—and the centuries—continues to be an asset and continues to be needed. It also continues to be somewhat unique as a store. It's a co-op. It is not run for profit. It's run for the benefit of its members, who receive a 2 percent discount on all purchases. (Members, who now number over 100, pay an annual fee of $20 per family and volunteer time to help run the store.) But anyone can shop there. And why wouldn't they? It's ten miles one way to get to the next nearest grocery store. That's a long way to go for a quart of milk, never mind a hot, homemade blueberry scone. For its part, the Vermont Preservation Trust may have uncharacteristically inherited a store, but it seems to have been a good fit for all parties.

"Yes, we still own the real estate," says Bruhn. "But they are making it work for real in North Shrewsbury; they're doing a fabulous job."

One has to think that Marjorie Pierce would be happy with how things have turned out.

"This is what she really wanted to happen," says Deinzer. "She didn't want it to be lost, she didn't want it to become a museum; she wanted it to remain a store for the community. And it is."

Harrisville General Store

The tiny village of Harrisville (Cheshire County), New Hampshire, owes its name and the name of its general store to the Harris family, who in turn owed its fortune to the unique abundance of water power here in this small pocket of New Hampshire's southwestern hills. The water from just small Goose Brook alone fell over 100 feet in just a quarter mile. By the early nineteenth century, that potential made the area irresistible for attracting mills that would add to New England's rapidly expanding textile industry. The Harris

Photo by Ted Reinstein

family (and later the Colony family) didn't merely create a cluster of woolen mills, they established an entire small village to surround and serve the mill complex, which included storehouses, offices, and homes (including boardinghouses and tenements). Because it was arduous, especially in winter, to travel even the short three miles to Dublin, New Hampshire, or the tougher ten miles to larger Peterborough, the mill village also included a general store to provide basic necessities to its workers and residents.

Photo by Ted Reinstein

In time, the textile mills of New England would dominate American woolen production. And in time, the descendants of those same mill owners would abandon the very region that had made them wealthy. They fled the riverbanks of the mighty Merrimack, the Blackstone, and the Androscoggin, first chasing cheaper production to the American south, then deserting their own country entirely for even cheaper costs overseas. Across New England, from Bangor to the Berkshires, from Manchester south to the former twin textile colossuses of Lawrence and Lowell, barely a century of production and prosperity was followed by decades of decline, then despair, as mills and factories that once anchored cities and entire regions with jobs and good futures closed down, one after another, often unmooring those same cities amidst rising unemployment and all the social ills that come with it.

But in little Harrisville, New Hampshire, something different happened. Not that it was ultimately spared some of the same experience that so many other New England mill towns went through. In 1970, the Cheshire Mills filed for bankruptcy. But by hanging on as long as it did, it had managed to preserve an early nineteenth-century New England mill village in its authentic, original, unchanged form. That makes Harrisville entirely unique. It also presented a pressing problem: what to do now that the mills—which had defined the town and employed most of its residents—would go silent and close for good. The town's

Photo courtesy of Historic Harrisville

response was to acknowledge that its unique history was also its best hope for the future.

Historic Harrisville, Inc. (HHI) was formed to preserve and renovate the mill buildings in hopes of attracting new businesses and creating new jobs as well as a new revenue stream for the town. Today, while the village itself looks nearly unchanged from vintage photos of its working mill days, those buildings now house a variety of contemporary businesses, artists' studios, affordable housing, a post office, and a daycare center.

But one building in Harrisville is still functioning in the same role it has since the early mill days—its general store. To be sure, its run has not been without periods when it was closed for a while, and it has survived sometimes in fits and starts, when villagers had to wonder if the lights that were out would ever go on again. When Historic Harrisville began its work, the store was privately owned. As 2000 approached, the then-owner sought permissions that would have allowed him to make significant changes to the original 1838 part of the building—essentially losing the original building as it had existed—this despite the building having National Historic Landmark status.

"There are only about 2,500 or so such buildings in the country, so any loss would have been a big loss—both for Harrisville and its standing as a landmark," says Linda Willett, who was hired by Historic Harrisville shortly after its founding in 1971. Today she is its executive director.

"It was clear to all of us that we simply could not allow that to happen to the store. Reviving it with its history intact was a major part of our operating plan for the village, and we realized we had to whatever we could to save it."

Photo by Ted Reinstein

They did. In 2000, Historic Harrisville purchased the store and set about a major rehab of the building. The idea was to bring it back fully to what it had been and to the role it had long played in the village.

"It really is a community need," says Willett. "These stores serve as general stores in these small places for basic needs, but they're also informal gathering places that the people who live here depend on, and it has gone beyond that in Harrisville."

Photo by Melissa Boulanger Photography

HHI was also deeply involved in several large mill projects with neither the resources nor the interest in taking over the store, so the plan was to find a new "owner" who would lease the store and manage it himself. There was a succession of such managers over a decade or so; alas, the store's success was spotty, depending on who was running it. And in truth, it was—and isn't—easy for anyone interested in actually making a living at it.

"It is a very difficult business," sighs Willett. "We have tourists in the summer, then in the winter the numbers plummet, the margins are so small."

Historic Harrisville realized it would need to find the right mix of someone willing to take on the challenge who also bought into the larger "mission" of preserving and maintaining this beloved community institution. The right mix seems to have been found, and just in time for the store's 175th anniversary.

Until recently, the store was managed by Laura Carden, whom many credit for the store's rebirth as an active, vital, and exciting center of the village again. Genuinely good, homemade food, not just dependably hot coffee, became a prime draw. Carden's mom, an established baker, joined her daughter, and their homemade cider donuts became a not-to-be-missed item. A strong emphasis was placed on locally sourced food, from produce and dairy to meat and poultry. A popular T-shirt from the store has a chicken on the front with the store's name and simply the word "Local" on the back.

"We try hard for our food to be local, and believe me, people really want local that's really local," says Phil Gargan, as he smiles. "People will come in and say, 'Do you have any of Dierdre's eggs?' Not just any local eggs—*Dierdre's* eggs!!"

Gargan and Samantha Rule are the current comanagers of the Harrisville General Store. Rule knew about the store because her son had gone to the Harrisville Children's Center. Gargan was born in Rhodesia and emigrated to the United States in 2012, when he and his family settled in Harrisville.

"For me, as an outsider," says Gargan, "it was a great way to get involved in the community."

Historic Harrisville saw a good fit with the pair. Rule, a graduate of the New England Culinary Institute and former chef for Peterborough's McDowell Artist Colony, was also mentored by the store's former manager, Laura Carden. Gargan's background is in filmmaking and management, so the roles mesh well. And both seem to understand what makes the store both a special challenge and a special place.

"It's more than a general store," says Gargan. "People come in and meet here, they play Scrabble, they run into their friends and neighbors; it's like another home that way."

But like any home, it takes upkeep and commitment to keep it going. The store is one of the few local employment opportunities; there's a paid staff of twelve, but plenty more pitch in, too.

"It really is a community endeavor," says Gargan. "We could never do it without all the volunteers. And also having Historic Harrisville very invested in the store's survival is huge for us and the town."

Even with that investment and all the volunteers, it's no cakewalk. The store sits in the middle of the historic mill village, atop Church Hill. It is not on any major route; it's not even on a well-traveled road.

"That makes it a destination store," admits Rule. "You have to know about it, and you have to want to come here."

And people do. In summer, it can get mobbed. Visitors from as far away as South Carolina, Florida, and California pop in for a coffee, a sandwich, a cider donut, and a taste of rare authenticity that makes a long detour well worth it for many.

Every Friday in summer, there's a local farmers' market outside the store. Once a month, there is a ticketed, themed dinner, and the store is transformed. Local artists supply original artwork for the walls, there are book readings, and every month the local Apple Hill Music School drops by to rehearse a piece they are working on.

"I love to see people's reactions," states Gargan. "You'll walk in and find a string quartet playing in the middle of the store."

In winter, though, it's a lot quieter.

"In winter, you might go for an hour and one person comes in." Gargan nods soberly. "It's not easy—seven days a week for both of us, very intensive."

Meanwhile, the store forges ahead, a unique blend of long-ago history, and the living, beating heart of present-day Harrisville.

"For us, for any general store like us to survive, it must be a center of the community," says Gargan. "It doesn't matter if it's a community of fishermen, farmers, or Scrabble-heads, but it must be a center of the community."

If it also makes the best BLT you've ever had (it does), that is truly icing on the cake.

After Tragedy—The Heart of a Town

Newtown sits in southwest Connecticut. It's not small—its population in 2010 was over 27,000—but it is close to some larger cities and is today a quiet bedroom community for a number of them. Founded in 1705, it's old. One can see the span of centuries in the range of period styles of the handsome clapboard homes, from Colonial to Colonial Revival, to Victorian. Its Main Street is classic New England Americana: rows of proud old maples and elms that line the way, a tall white church steeple, the Cyrenius H. Booth Library, an equally proud town flagpole flying Old Glory right there in the middle of it all where it can't be missed. Just past the flagpole sits another proud piece of Americana, the Newtown General Store.

The store first opened its doors in 1847. Other than at church, it was the only place in town at which one could count on running into neighbors. It still is. Residents buy their morning coffee here and stop by for a chat, teenagers head over during a break from school to order a sandwich for lunch.

Photo by Art Donahue Photography

In summer, softball league players jam into the store to grab a snack before the game. Locals with a bit more time sit and have dessert at one of the few tables scattered inside the store, the original wooden floorboards creaking underneath their feet. The look and feel of the 1,400-square-foot store remains much like it was in 1847. "That's intentional," says Peter Leone, who has owned the store since 2000. Leone calls his store "a kind of community center" for Newtown.

Photo by Art Donahue Photography

That was never more painfully true than on December 14, 2012.

On that unspeakable nightmare of a day, twenty schoolchildren and six adult staff members were fatally shot by an armed intruder at the Sandy Hook elementary school. The nation, and the world, recoiled in horror. But in this small town, the victims were not merely names on the news, they were neighbors, and the shock and grief were staggering. As after 9/11, townspeople felt a need to reach out and comfort and to be comforted. There were vigils. Some gathered at churches. And some gathered at the Newtown General Store.

A few days after the shootings, Peter Leone took a call from a 911 dispatcher in Los Angeles. The dispatcher said that he sympathized with what people in town must be going through and offered to pay for $100 worth of coffee for customers coming to the store. Leone quickly typed up the man's name and where he was from and posted it on a sign on the counter so that people could see that even in the face of such suffering, there was kindness.

In the days that followed, the phone started ringing off the hook. People called the store and wanted to buy the residents of the town something, anything. They bought breakfast sandwiches, cookies, and candy. The store received calls for platters of cookies and sandwiches to be donated to police and first responders. Leone says he received calls from every corner of the country, including Alaska. A serviceman in Afghanistan called to make a donation. Leone had to bring in family members just to handle the daily volume of calls. And with each call, he faithfully recorded the names of the donors and where they were from, dutifully posting the signs in the store. The national news media came to the

store to interview Leone. They took pictures of the signs that now wallpapered the interior of this little store, built at time when mass killings only happened in war.

As the days turned into weeks, the calls into the store began to slow to a trickle. Still, it took Leone almost two months to fulfill all the donations that had been logged. Now it's five years. The sadness will forever be a part of this pretty town now. But it doesn't define it. The stately trees and handsome homes and sturdy little store and—above all—the close-knit community, all existed before tragedy struck. It exists still. Stronger. For Peter Leone, his Main Street perch helped make that message clear.

"The overwhelming outpouring of emotional support I saw reminds me that although there is a lot of bad in the world, it's a truly amazing thing to witness the positive, warm, endearing side of human nature."

Written on the walls, one at a time, in a little, old general store.

Barnard General Store

(BARNARD, VT)

Established in 1832

When the Barnard General Store opened in 1832, Andrew Jackson was president. When it closed in 2012, Barack Obama was. When it reopened, Obama was still president. Needless to say, there's a story there. Clearly, Barnard, Vermont, is not fond of being without its general store for long.

Photo courtesy of the Charles Danforth Library, Barnard, VT

A little bit about Barnard. It's a small town (population 947 in 2010), located almost smack in the center of Vermont, a bit closer to the New Hampshire border to the east than the New York border to its west. It's also nearly equidistant from the Massachusetts border to the south and the Canadian border to the north. But none of this "stuck in the middle" stuff should lead one to think that residents here are necessarily all mild-mannered, middle-of-the-road milquetoasts without strong feelings or opinions.

On my first visit to the general store, an older gent sitting on the front porch (presumably seeing my camera and telltale reporter's notebook poking from my back pocket) called out to me, "Hey, I'll give you all the dirt on everything here—I'll tell you stories you won't believe."

Nothing middle of the road there.

At the western end of the town's most recognizable landmark, Silver Lake, at a four-way stop, is perhaps the town's second-most recognizable landmark. It's a fairly simple and unassuming two-story wood building. It also looks and feels like the quintessential country store—wide, unfinished wood floors, short aisles of groceries, small tables clustered at one corner, complete with an old-fashioned ice-cream counter. Outside, a front porch faces out on the pretty lake.

The Barnard General Store has occupied this spot for 185 years. But in 2012, the then-owners found themselves in financial trouble. It could have been the double hit of Hurricane Irene followed by a ski season with no snow. It could have been just living on the edge for too long; it could have been other things, but the main thing was that the debt got too large, and before the town knew what hit it, the store closed. Folks were devastated.

"There was a huge hole in the community," Barnard resident Linda Treash told a local TV station shortly afterward. "It was a common place for people to meet to gather and just catch up. There has just been that loss."

Another resident, Meg Johnson, summed it up more succinctly: "It is the heartbeat of the town."

And it had stopped beating. So townspeople decided to do something, to bring the store back to life and, with it, a vital organ of their town. They formed the Barnard Community Trust (BCT) and reached out for guidance and assistance from the Preservation Trust of Vermont. Smart moves all. In a year, they raised over half a million dollars, much of it from local donations.

"It really ran the gamut," says Tom Platner, president of BCT. "We raised everything from $3.95 from a kid who had a lemonade stand, to families who gave us $200,000. But they all knew it wasn't just about a building; this is an important place."

The BCT was able to secure a mortgage and buy the store. The doors were reopened only a year later, while new full-time owners were sought and—thanks to Paul Bruhn of the PTV—found.

Joe Minerva and Jillian Bradley grew up together on Long Island. Fast forward past school and a decade or so, and the couple was living in Vermont, helping manage the Richmond Market in Burlington. Bruhn, helping Barnard in the hunt for new store owners, approached them. Minerva and Bradley actually were all set to buy a small supermarket and go off on their own. The sale fell through, Bruhn pounced, the couple visited the Barnard General Store, and something clicked.

"Honestly, it sounds crazy," says Bradley, standing behind the deli counter of the store on a lovely summer Sunday afternoon four years later. "But we walked in here, looked around for a bit, then looked at each other, and said, 'This is why the other thing fell through.'"

So the store ended up being closed for only a year. Minerva and Bradley signed a thirty-year lease on the store ("Well . . . ," Bradley smiles sheepishly), and the Barnard Community Trust maintains ownership of the building itself.

While the couple knew something about management (Bradley's degree is in hospitality), they had no cooking experience.

"We improvised a lot for a bit," laughs Bradley. "I went to a couple of local guys who had a restaurant and asked them to give me a one-hour lesson in cooking eggs."

Today, locals flock to the fresh buttermilk pancakes on Sunday morning. They serve breakfast and lunch every day. Bradley is the grocery manager; Jillian runs the deli like a veteran diner jockey and is the face of the store.

Photo by Art Donahue Photography

"I know the first names of all my locals," she says. "Well . . . faces for sure, even if I don't [know] the name."

As for the local guys who gather for breakfast Monday through Friday at the big round table in the front, no names are necessary.

"They don't even have to order—I know what each of them wants."

It's not all a snap. The hardworking couple routinely puts in twelve-hour days, seven days a week. They're closed only on Christmas. For the first two-and-a-half years, the couple lived above the store. More recently, they bought a nearby house of their own.

"There were days I would say to Joe, 'Wow—I haven't left this building the entire week!'"

Technically, the store is open on Thanksgiving. But that's only so that Joe and Jillian can have their extended families come to the store to celebrate. They fire up the woodstove, cook up a huge meal in the kitchen, lay it all out on the store's counter, and enjoy the holiday in what is either their first or second home, depending on how they look at it on any given week.

"It's a lot of work," concedes Bradley. "I have more gray than I should have at twenty-seven!"

But the couple can—and does—take deep satisfaction in the fact that a beloved place in Barnard is back. And they are a big part of keeping it alive.

"It means different things to different people," says Platner. "To some people, they can get gas and lunch; to some people, it's where they meet; to summer tourists, it's a beautiful place on the lake. But it's the heart of our community; there wouldn't be much of a village without it."

THE UNSINKABLES

As physical buildings, general stores are vulnerable to the same dangers that can do in your house: fire, flood, hurricane, tornado, or simple benign neglect. Because the general stores in this book are all in New England, tornadoes are not typically a threat. Because they are all surviving and well supported, neither is benign neglect. That leaves fire and flood. And those are cataclysms that have touched both of the remarkable stores that follow here. Granted, 200-year-old buildings are no match for Mother Nature. But it's not easy to burn or wash away centuries of tradition—especially when the community that's created it is committed to coming to the rescue.

The Phoenix: Putney General Store

(PUTNEY, VT)

Established in 1799

General stores have been described in many ways. Some are very old, some have very colorful histories, some are regional landmarks, a special few are beloved as the true beating heart of their communities. In Putney, Vermont, all these apply.

A general merchandise store has sat on the same spot above Sacketts Brook in Putney for close to 200 years. That's a lot of time to get attached. By 1799, what had started as a grist mill was already operating as a store. Naturally, through the decades, centuries really, there has been more than a dozen owners: Griffin, Chandler, Keyes, Britton, Baker, Hewitt, Kelley, Corser, Cummings, Fickett, Fairchild. And that partial roll call only takes

Photo by Art Donahue Photography

us up to the 1970s and the period when the name Putney General Store first took hold. The store changed hands twice more between then and 2006. Still, having started in the eighteenth century, by the beginning of the twenty-first, it could be said that the Putney General Store had seen its way through the nation's infancy, the Civil War, the Depression, two world wars, the social upheaval of the sixties, and 9/11.

But history, alas, isn't fireproof.

On the night of May 3, 2008, flames broke out in the store, possibly the result of some faulty wiring in the attic. By the time it was over, the store was still standing, but the interior damage was extensive. For the owners, it was financially impossible to do anything but gather their losses and get out.

"We had hoped the owners would rebuild," says Lyssa Papazian, president of the Putney Historical Society. "But they just couldn't do it."

Photo courtesy of Putney Historical Society

After 200 years, people in Putney weren't content to simply gaze at the charred and gutted hulk of what had been a living and vital cornerstone of their town's history. So they didn't.

In November 2008, amid a complicated series of state, private, and federal grants, the Putney Historical Society was able to purchase the store. Within a few months, rebuilding had begun.

As Papazian recalls, on the day the building's new roof trusses were lifted into place, cars passing by spontaneously stopped and honked their horns; people clapped and cheered.

"As a general store—and like so many other true general stores in Vermont—that place was the center of Putney's community," says Paul Bruhn, executive director of the Preservation Trust of Vermont. "In taking on what it did, the Putney Historical Society understood that."

While the fire that had gutted the store was never officially ruled "suspicious," there were questions. But there would be no questions or mystery about what happened a year and a half later. On November 1, 2009—incredibly—the store was struck by a second fire. This time, accelerants were found. Arson. After the store was very nearly lost to fire the first time, this time there was no "nearly." The store was burned down to its foundation stones. Like an ashen grave site, a soot-covered dirt lot strewn with blackened rubble was all there was to mark where the store had stood. It was gone.

"It was like being punched in the gut," says Papazian, looking off into the far distance as if recalling a painful family tragedy. In a way, it was. "Everyone in this town, really, was invested at that point. It was a feeling of being in shock. Just shock."

Residents, reeling, found themselves staring at the smoldering ruins of their store with disbelief. They gathered in a spontaneous candlelight vigil. There really was the sense of a death in the family.

"People wanted to do something, but no one knew what to do. We were like in mourning," says Papazian.

The memorial service just happened; no one remembers planning it. People gathered in a 200-year-old building, sitting on 100-year-old horse-hair cushions. They told stories and shared memories. It wasn't made clear in any way at the time, but there was an unspoken sense that, one way or another, they were going to rebuild their store. Again.

"If we didn't rebuild again, that meant that an arsonist was in charge here," says former teacher John Caldwell, who moved to Putney as a boy in 1941, then moved back in 1953. "We weren't going to let some guy drive us away."

"I remember getting the call the night of the second fire. Lyssa called; it was very upsetting," says Bruhn. "I went down the next day. We had originally planned to meet with five or six people who'd worked most closely with the store. But as more and more people found out about the meeting, more and more people showed up. There must have been at least thirty. We had an amazing conversation. There was a clear feeling of 'We will not let our community be defined by an arsonist.'"

Photo courtesy of Putney Historical Society

But for the time being, it was the onset of winter, and nothing could be done until spring. The cold, dark months that followed gave residents a grim image of what life without their venerable general store would be. Where once in winter there had been the warm, welcoming store lights on the corner and inside the promise of hot coffee and a friendly face to greet, now there was just . . . darkness. A cold and unfamiliar void.

"The town seemed to turn into a ghost town, honestly," says Caldwell.

There were no tumbleweeds blowing down Main Street, but that's only because Putney is in Vermont, not Arizona. For the first time, Putney's other businesses, from pizza shops to dry-cleaners, got a bitter taste of what their town would be like without the sturdy, stalwart store on the corner. It was suddenly and unsettlingly clear to all the other merchants that the general store was the anchor for everything else—the people who dropped in the general store to grab a coffee or a carton of milk also stopped in at their

Photo by Ted Reinstein

businesses. Without the general store, it was as if people wanted to simply avoid the town's center. Everyone was hurting.

Papazian physically shudders in recalling that winter after the second fire. "It was so dark all of a sudden on that corner, it was awful, it was sad—we needed to have some light!"

Papazian and some others strung some lights on the security fence that surrounded the lot where the store had stood. Someone hung a big picture of a phoenix. A sign went up on the fence: "We don't need a building—WE are the general store!"

The phoenix was rising. Again.

The long, cold winter finally gave way to spring, and with it came the rebirth the town so badly needed. Local timber was donated. A local sawyer donated his time to cut it. Financial donations of all kinds and from all quarters poured in. The rebuilding effort rode a tide of sheer will and positive energy to quick completion.

Photo by Art Donahue Photography

"That took extraordinary effort on the part of the community, to face fire not once but twice," marvels Bruhn. "I have always thought that, more than anything, Putney is about perseverance."

Today, Putney has its store back. The town has its beating heart back. In a way, the roof that rose over the new store seemed to cover the town as well in its sheltering sense of wholeness again.

The coffee gets poured all day, the deli counter hums with activity, people pull up and dart in for a loaf of bread or a carton of milk, the regulars meet up, and warm waves and greetings are exchanged throughout the day inside and out.

Upstairs at the store, John Caldwell and his buddies are home again. The Viagra Club is back in session. Thankfully, the world has a half dozen or so older guys prepared each day to solve its problems. Or at least watch the cars go by.

"After the fire, we still met up and stood on the street drinking coffee," he laughs. "Now we're back inside the store where we belong. Hey, we kept the faith."

For her part, Lyssa Papazian has learned to temper her happiness about the store's revival with the nagging and sober-minded reality that life is not easy for general stores, even for those that have come back to life. Twice.

"It's back to being an anchor of the town," she says, sitting on the store's front porch on a sunny October afternoon. "But the future . . ."

She shrugs, smiles wanly, and spreads her hands slightly, palms up. For now, the Putney Historical Society continues to own the store. The present operator also runs a pharmacy on the second floor. But the realities are what they are. Putney, a town of about 3,000, has no ski area nearby to feed tourists into its Main Street in winter. It can be bleak for business.

Photo by Art Donahue Photography

"Our goal has been to offer low rent and just keep the debt off of the operator," Papazian says. "Still, the margins are so thin, and the store is hanging on by a thread."

If and when a new operator is needed, the PHS will step up and try to find one. They remain committed to keeping the town's general store going. After everything the town has been through to keep the store alive, it's hard to imagine giving up now.

"Meanwhile, next time you're here, who knows?" Papazian laughs. "You might find me behind the counter!"

"Whatever it takes, right?" I offer.

"Whatever it takes."

Fortunately, this phoenix has a flock of friends, faithful and true, who are determined to keep it aloft. Whatever it takes.

Robie's Country Store

(HOOKSETT, NH)

Established in 1822

Interstate 93 runs clear up most of New Hampshire, from the Massachusetts border up past the north country of the White Mountains. Just south of Concord, New Hampshire, sits the town of Hooksett. Most of the waves of travelers and motorists on I-93 who pass through the Hooksett highway toll area are headed farther north, to the state's popular lakes region in summer and to equally popular ski areas in winter. And that is as close to Hooksett as most people get. Which, until relatively recently, included me. Which is really a damn shame. Because getting off the highway in Hooksett and weaving your way down the hill to the landmark at #9 River Street is well worth getting to your ski vacation an hour later than planned.

Robie's Country Store has occupied its spot along the Merrimack River since it was built in 1822 (in more than one physical incarnation, though). In time, the railroad would run alongside it as well. It was well situated for commerce. (The interstate wouldn't be built until the 1960s.) Early on, there was a dock out on the riverbank where barges could unload goods directly at the store.

Photo by Ted Reinstein

Photo courtesy of the Robie Collection

The Robie family didn't always own it, it just seems that way. They began operating the store in 1887, and it remained in control of the family for over 100 years, passed down from father to son like a prized family heirloom, which it was. But it was also one prized by the broader community, too, as much like a town hall or community center as a general store. (The store actually predates the Hooksett Town Hall.) Town meetings were held there, election results were posted there, and, until 1975, it also served as a post office.

All of which is even more impressive considering the building was out of action for the town on more than one occasion. As in destroyed. In 1857, a fire consumed the store. It was rebuilt. In 1906, a second fire once again destroyed it. Once more, it was rebuilt.

But fire wasn't the store's only nemesis.

"If it wasn't fire, it was water!" exclaims Robert Schroeder, a genial, soft-spoken man in his late sixties and president of the Robie's Country Store Historic Preservation

Corporation, a community nonprofit that now owns the store. "The store has withstood several floods from the river; sometimes it seems like it has nine lives."

Schroeder was a close friend of Lloyd and Dot Robie, the last of four generations of the family to own and run the store. Schroeder and all of Hooksett would have been happy to have Lloyd and Dot run the store forever. Sometimes it seemed as if they might. It certainly seemed as if the couple was as much a permanent fixture of the store as the creaky wood floor and the walls covered with decades of political mementos.

Given the lure of the New Hampshire presidential primary every four years, diners and general stores across the Granite State all have walls similarly plastered with signed pictures of smiling (and often oddly optimistic) candidates. Not every whistle stop in the state, though, can boast of figuring in a future president's nickname.

"Robie's has always been a stop for political candidates," says Schroeder. "But Carter put it permanently on the map for future candidates."

In 1976, then-Georgia governor and democratic presidential candidate Jimmy Carter was on his way to Concord for a larger campaign event. Passing the Robie's store, Carter's staff decided to pop in and say hello.

"It was early in the morning, I was making coffee, and Lloyd was working in the post office section of the store," Dot Robie later told a reporter for the *Boston Globe.*

"Carter came in the back door, asked if Mr. Robie was around, and I called out, 'Mr. Robie, someone's here to see you.' Carter walked over and said, 'Mr. Robie, I'm Jimmy Carter and I'm running for president.' Well, Mr. Robie was nearly deaf, he was wearing two hearing aids even then. He didn't hear him and said, 'Jimmy *who*?' So that's where that started and it stuck with Carter."

Photo by Ted Reinstein

It certainly did. Twenty-five years later, visitors to the Jimmy Carter Library & Museum in Atlanta could view an exhibit called "From 'Jimmy Who?' to President."

Amid worsening health issues, Lloyd and Dot Robie decided to close the store in 1997. They approached their friend and former Realtor Bob Schroeder.

"They needed to retire," says Schroeder. "But they were very adamant that they didn't want the store to go away. So the idea we settled on was to form a nonprofit to buy the store and, hopefully, control its use."

A quick succession of operators had mixed success with running the venerable store. One of them negligently allowed the pipes to freeze, causing them to burst, and giving Schroeder and others a chilling flashback to earlier woes (fire, flood) that had historically plagued the store.

In January 2016, the store's current operators took over. Husband and wife Amber and Josh Enright, both chefs, had a catering business. They took one visit to Robie's and loved the space and the political history immediately. Amber Enright said she felt "like it was home."

"You are buying Robie's role as a country store," says Josh. "Some of the previous recent owners seemed to just want to run a business out of the store."

The couple has made it clear that they want Robie's to be both a community store stocked with groceries as well as a café open for breakfast and lunch. Locals enthusiastically drop in for Sunday morning pancakes. Once a month, the store offers a farm-to-table dinner complete with wine pairings. The Enrights are also running their catering business, Roots Café & Catering, from the store.

"It's all about local," says Josh. He and Amber, both New Hampshire natives, know what that means. "Local farmers, local produce, local New Hampshire products. It's time-consuming, but thankfully we have a lot of family around, and we get a lot of help."

Photos by Ted Reinstein

The emphasis on good food is drawing new customers, many from farther away. Still, Amber sometimes finds herself appreciating some of the same simple joys that have drawn folks to the store for centuries.

"People will stop in, maybe with their kids, they'll get candy or an ice cream, and sit outside by the river."

The really good things about a great general store don't change. Come hell or high water.

HONEY, I BOUGHT THE STORE

Some general stores have survived by being passed down between generations of own-ers as an enduring family business. Others have required a long line of succeeding owners to stay open. Why does someone today—anyone—go and buy a general store (especially one that's been closed for any length of time)? That's a very good question. After all, there are easier things to do with one's hard-earned money and time. Like, drill for oil in your backyard. And yet, thankfully, there are people who have indeed decided to buy a general store, which has kept those stores alive and surviving. For now. For the folks who follow here, it has not exactly been like striking oil. But there's been something precious about it all the same.

Marshfield Hills General Store

(MARSHFIELD, MA)

Established in 1953

You might be familiar with actor Steve Carell from his work on the television series *The Office* and in films such as *Little Miss Sunshine* and *The 40-Year-Old Virgin.* But in Marshfield, Massachusetts, he's perhaps more famous for his role in a 160-year-old revival.

Marshfield, in Plymouth County, is a quiet Boston bedroom community on the city's South Shore. It takes its name from the many salt marshes that dot the area along the ocean. While there is rich Early American and nineteenth-century maritime history here, I've always been most impressed by the peculiar fact that this town, with a population of just over 25,000, boasts six separate zip codes. And one longtime, beloved general store.

There has been a retail establishment on the same spot on Prospect Street here since at least 1853, when Elisha Hall opened for business, sharing a proud, old two-story building with the local post office. During the Civil War, Union Army uniforms were hand-sewn in an upstairs room. Over the next fifty years, half a dozen different owners kept the store in business to varying degrees of success. But the store stood. And today, older folks in Marshfield recall with relish what a treat it was on a warm summer night to be taken to the store to pick out a pocketful of penny candy.

In 2008, then-owner Sherry Campbell Bechtold (also author of *My Life at the Marshfield Hills General Store*) was ready to relinquish her "turn" as caretaker of the store. She wanted to sell it and was determined to find a new owner equally committed to continuing the store and its tradition. But 2008 through 2009 was not a particularly auspicious period in which to find a buyer; America was sliding into the single worst economic downturn since the Great Depression.

"It was so depressing to think of it closing for good," says Marshfield resident Tish Vivado. "All the kids who live here would have literally no place to go."

At the time, Vivado had lived in Marshfield for about a decade. Her own kids had already become devoted regulars of the store. (Think candy. Lots of candy.) She was

Photo by J. Michael Sullivan

crestfallen about the prospect of losing her favorite place on Prospect. In October 2008, she went out to Los Angeles to visit her sister, Nancy, and famous brother-in-law, Steve, and told them that the Marshfield store was for sale. They asked her to find out more details immediately. She did.

"I was a history major in college; I love history," says Steve Carell, speaking with me from his Los Angeles home in 2016. "I love that Civil War uniforms were sewn in the rooms above the store in Marshfield. Also, it seemed like such a gathering place in the community, and it seemed like such a shame for a place like that to close; it would likely never reopen."

Carell did more than lament from afar. He and Nancy ponied up over half a million dollars and became the new owners of a general store.

"I had never imagined owning a general store," Carell admits. "It wasn't a lifelong dream of mine."

But it also wasn't something completely outside his life, either. As a child growing up just west of Boston in Acton, Massachusetts, Carell has fond memories of visiting a long-gone general store there named Boker's.

Photo by Ted Reinstein

"The sweetest old man ran it; he was a purveyor of everything, had a gas pump out front," recalls Carell. "It was a magical place to me. I loved it, and it seemed like a natural gathering place, too, and that always stayed with me."

Although Carell and his family live full-time in Los Angeles, they spend time every summer in Marshfield. So, in addition to his fondness for history, there was also a natural local connection for him in purchasing the store. Vivado became the store's general manager, and the team set about making extensive renovations and improvements to it.

Today, looking back at becoming involved with the store, Vivado jokes about her lack of retail experience (she had been registrar at Tufts University Medical School).

"I thought, What am I doing? I even hate shopping. Honestly, I really do."

For his part, Carell was very certain and specific about certain marching orders.

"He said to me, 'Just fill it,' recalls Vivado. "He wanted it to look full of stuff, fun stuff, useful stuff, just inviting but familiar to people who knew it, too."

Vivado jumped into her new role with a lot of gusto if little guidance.

"I had no idea what I was doing," Vivado offers, sitting on the front porch on a warm, early June evening. "The previous owners were absolutely lovely, bless them, and they loved this place, but they had no real system to share with me. They told me, 'Oh, we don't even count the change.' And I thought, Um, what?? I made plenty of mistakes, but you figure it out. For instance, I figured out that kids do not like yellow candy!"

Even without a clear guide from the former owners, the store's legendary candy section proved to be something of a guiding totem for the new owners.

"You know, granted, it's a little hokey," says Carell, "but the thought of having a place where kids can go, safely, where you can take your kids, get some candy, sit on the porch . . . "

Things began to take shape at the store. Its smallish 900 square feet does indeed feel full. There are simple staples and groceries, lots of little gift items, and a surprisingly extensive wine and beer section. (No hard liquor, though, or cigarettes or lottery tickets.) And, of course, a buzzing coffee corner to cater to the morning regulars.

"Anyone can come in and get anything," Vivado says. "Kids can get candy, adults can get wine and coffee, and tourists can get mementos and local things, too."

Conscientious general store owners know they are also stewards of history and they need to balance that responsibility with many other factors, including running a successful business. It's not an easy juggling act, especially when the owner is a self-avowed lover of history.

"We didn't want to open it as a museum," Carell says. "We wanted to keep the element of the candy section, make a store as comprehensive as we could make it, but with simplicity. I mean, there's a post office next door—why not sell postcards so people can get one, get a coffee, write one out on the porch, then go next door to mail it?"

In speaking with Carell, it's clear that he has a more expansive sense of what general stores can mean to a community. And what it can mean for a community to lose one.

"You lose a vital gathering spot, and those are rare—a place of true communication, not electronic communication, real, face-to-face communication. That's what I love. To lose those things is to lose an innocence that this country once had. It's a place to slow down. People yearn for that and for that chance to communicate more innocently like that."

Carell's annual visits to Marshfield now spread excited murmurs throughout the town. People drive by the store, hoping to catch a glimpse or, even better, to be there when he stops in. He does drop by to check in on things and is generally happy to greet customers and pose for selfies. He may be a summer visitor, but it is his store, after all.

"My wife and I thought more in terms of buying it for the town, not for us," he says. "When we're back in Marshfield, people pull us aside and say just, 'Thank you. Thank you for doing that.' And that feels really good."

Photo by Ann Francis

Fern's

(CARLISLE, MA)
Established in 1844

Of all the stories in this particular chapter, this is the only one in which an about-to-be general store owner actually uttered the words "Honey, I bought the store."

Okay, technically, as Larry Bearfield recounts, his actual words were "Honey, we're going to buy the store in the town village center." The main thing is, they ended up doing just that. The other crazy thing is, it wasn't even for sale at the time.

"We were both burnt out, both looking for a change," says Bearfield of himself and his wife and partner, Robin Emerson. "Besides," he says with a playful, sarcastic grin, "how hard could it be?"

Photo by Nancy Pattison Roberts

The easy part was that their out-of-the-blue offer for the store in 2003 was accepted. Hard work, business savvy, and creative skills were not lacking for the couple. Larry and Robin had spent most of their professional lives in advertising and promotion. They'd had their own ad agency for thirty years, but commuting back and forth into Boston had gotten old.

Photo by Ted Reinstein

"We were looking to get out," says Bearfield flatly, as Emerson nods in agreement.

Once out, and now newly minted owners of a store that would need to reopen under their new vision, they had to decide what exactly that vision would be. There had been a general store on the same spot since 1844, but the brand-new stewards were determined to put their own stamp on its history, to create their own perfect general store. So they took a year and set about traveling around New England, visiting a variety of general stores, hoping to find that one, ideal model for what would become their own. They never found all that they were after under one roof but rather were drawn to different elements and qualities from all the different stores they visited.

"We realized we'd have to create a composite," says Bearfield.

And in many ways, perhaps Fern's represents just that—a successful blending of many of the diverse qualities that one finds in a good general store, starting with the front door itself: Bells jangle as it opens. Small touch. Big symbol.

"Front door bells remind people of that friendly, local store feeling," says Emerson, looking about the store. "We have fresh cookies baking all day; the smell permeates."

There's a deli counter where patrons can order sandwiches and a small café that serves meals throughout the day. And coffee, never-ending coffee, offered in what seems to be the corner of the store where the real conversations happen.

Photo by Ted Reinstein

"I drive by every day and I stop in to get myself a cup of great coffee," says Peter King, a regular customer from neighboring Bedford. "This is where they really *do* know your name. I had a back operation recently, I came in, and they asked about my back. You just don't get that everywhere."

There's a grocery section that stocks the basics. ("We call it the 'Oh, my God, I forgot' section," Bearfield laughs.) Much of the fresh produce is locally sourced; 250 dozen eggs a month come from a local farm.

There is also an entire separate area that sells beer and wine and features wine tastings and a "Wine Learning Series" (it's unclear how graduates are judged). Getting the wine and beer section was not easy, either. Carlisle had been a "dry" town for 150 years. It took 6 years of committees and boards and meetings before the decision was reached to "un-dry" it.

"We elect the leader of the free world in one vote," laughs Bearfield. "But it takes six years to un-dry a town!"

There's a busy bakery. That fresh-baked cookie smell wafting from end to end of the store is real.

What's also clearly real is how invested the owners are in both this store and their town. Carlisle is a rural town, about 5,000 people. It's only 25 miles northwest of Boston, but it's spread out in hilly, green fields and horse farms. There are few neighborhoods of contained, straight streets, which makes for tough trick-or-treating. So Bearfield and Emerson made Fern's the town center for Halloween, with big spiders on the roof and tons of candy on the front porch for the taking. But as invested as the store's owners are, their customers seem to feel equally so.

"Our customers feel connected to us," Bearfield says. "They'll say, 'You know what you should do?' When would someone say that or feel like they could make a suggestion to a big supermarket chain? Our customers do that all the time. And we listen. They feel a real sense of ownership here."

The store has doubled in size since 2010. It's bigger but still feels homey, rustic, fun, and unpretentious.

"When we were renovating," Bearfield recalls, "the contractor said, 'We've got a problem—the door is a little off.' And I said, 'Hey, it's a country store, it doesn't really matter.'"

What does seem to matter is the fact that in this spread-out town with no other natural meeting place, there is one.

"Larry and Robin really have turned it into a genuine gathering place," says Margaret Krauss Skelly, a transplant to Carlisle. "When I first moved out here from Boston, it was really hard at first for me to connect with people. Now I often think, if only Fern's had been here, it would have been a lot easier."

One thing is for sure. In creating their "perfect" country store, Emerson and Bearfield may have drawn on a composite of all of their favorite qualities from other stores, but their creation feels like its own, unique example. Not bad for two store owners who'd never run a store before.

"Ever feel like 'This is a lot of work—what have we gotten ourselves into?'" I ask Robin. She throws her head back and laughs.

"Just in the beginning. But it passes."

Cornwall Country Market

(CORNWALL BRIDGE, CT)

Established in 1835

Connecticut is a state of interesting contrasts. In the south, Fairfield County is a succession of towns and cities on Long Island Sound, some gritty and urban, some leafy and affluent. But other corners of Connecticut are deeply rural, full of dense woods, rolling hills, and tidy farms. In northwestern Connecticut, the town of Cornwall lies less than ten miles from the New York State border. Hard by the Housatonic River, in the shadow of

Photo by Art Donahue Photography

Photo courtesy of James Shepard

Mohawk Mountain, you'll find the Cornwall Country Market. The store that stands today where Routes 4 and 7 meet represents a living link in a chain that goes back nearly 200 years.

In 1835, H.W. Breen's General Merchandise Store opened for business near the east end of a covered bridge. A century later, Breen's descendants decided to rebuild the store closer to a more modern bridge along the new highway. It's been there ever since, through a succession of families, each of whom exhibited remarkable longevity in a tough business. The Breens ran it until 1940, when it was sold and carried on as Monroe and O'dell's General Store for thirty more years. In the 1970s, it became Baird's General Store, and Bairds continued to run it until 2010. Alas, no owner along the way seemed to have been able to temporarily close just long enough to do the simple repair and upgrade work that more than a century and a half requires of a building at a certain point. From the limited water supply, to an outmoded electrical system, to a furnace that was described as a "museum piece," the store was itself now more of a local relic than a realistic business. Whoever bought it would be required to finally do all that modernizing and renovating that a long succession of owners had avoided. They'd also be required to make a certain leap of faith.

"It really started with dinner at my stepdad's," said James Shepard, who, along with his wife, Idella, had spent a long time in the food and hospitality industry. Too long, as far as they were concerned. "My history was in food service and bar management; my wife was coming from a catering background in Boston," says Shepard. "I had worked at a lot of corporations, and we were both sick of it—sixty-hour weeks for really nothing. We got hurt bad in the recession. We were sick of working for other people, we were just sick of the whole thing."

In other words, they were ready to take a leap.

"My stepfather lived in Cornwall and said come to dinner. He had this crazy idea because he knew we had looked at another store in the Cornwall area."

Shepard's stepfather was savvy about general stores and had done his homework. He had concluded that the problem for many new general-store owners was that rents were often very high and that the start-up and operating costs were often crippling. His idea? He would buy a building and renovate it for James and Idell, who would then be able to invest their savings in starting up the business end and creating a new version of an older store. The couple got a good deal on a property, but it needed a lot of work. After all, it was almost 200 years old, had a museum piece for a furnace, and had been neglected for years.

"We needed to fix what was broken," Shepard says. "We thought it might be closed for a couple of weeks; it took about six months."

The whole store was brought down to the studs, the floor plan was opened up, a porch was added, and the whole infrastructure was updated and improved. During the process, townspeople dropped by to say hi but also to register their own sense of ownership, however emotional and symbolic, about their longtime general store.

"Shortly before we opened, Idella and I were distressing wood boards," Shepard laughs. "A line of people were waiting to talk to us. They told us what they wanted and what they didn't want; we had to shoo them away, tell them we were never going to open unless they let us get back to work!"

On November 1, 2013, the new (and newly renamed) Cornwall Country Market opened. On my visit, they had recently celebrated their third anniversary.

"It was a big learning curve," Shepard says today. "We're the only food service place in town. We don't want to be lazy about that. The store had to look like a store not a convenience store. It took us a while to rebrand. But we know everybody, and everybody made sure they knew us."

It does seem that way. On a chilly morning just after Christmas, with light snow swirling in the air, a man waves to Shepard on entering the store, hearty greetings all around.

"At one time there were three different similar stores in the area; this is the last one standing, and it's so important," says Gordon Ridgway, Cornwall's first selectman, who points out that he is both a customer and a provider for the store. Ridgway owns a farm in town that sells maple syrup and dairy products to the store. He underscores just how important it is to keeping the store alive.

In January 2015, a local lumberyard burned in a huge fire that ultimately involved twenty area fire departments. Ridgway called and woke up Shepard in the middle of the night. The sleepy store owner turned on the store's lights and got food and coffee to nearly eighty cold and tired firemen.

"You can't put a price on what that means to a town," says Ridgway.

The store sits near the northwestern Connecticut section of the Appalachian Trail, and it's common in warmer months to see hikers sitting on the porch, enjoying a sandwich and a cold drink. An even more common sight (as in, daily) is the group of regulars in the cozy "dining area" off the main room where the deli and shelf goods are located.

"They really upped the quality of the food," says regular Larry Cunningham. "I've gained twenty-five pounds since they opened!"

Cunningham, sixty-six, bears a striking resemblance to Ernest Hemingway. He grew up just over the border in Amenia, New York, but lives next door to the store now. His dad ran a general store in Sharon, Connecticut. He knows the dedication and hard work it takes.

"James and Idella work like dogs, and that's what it takes, but everything they do is top shelf!"

Shepard doesn't dispute the dog part. "This isn't a job, it's a lifestyle. I am working tomorrow, I am working every day. We went through stages of wondering, What the hell was I thinking? But we've learned as we go. There are no secret launch codes. Don't over-promise. Deliver. It's knowing when one guy gets his *WSJ* with a buttered roll, another guy gets bacon, egg, and cheese. Make every customer know they are welcome."

It seems to work. As I am leaving, I introduce myself to a couple in camo gear getting into their truck, which I notice has New Hampshire plates. Turns out Allen and Trish Spicer have been bow-hunting nearby and dropped into the store to get some soup and warm up on this snowy morning. They definitely felt welcome.

"When we came in, there were no seats open," says Spicer. "The guys said, 'Hey, sit with us, we don't bite.' Actually, one of 'em said, 'Well, I bite.' And we laughed and met all new friends."

I'm guessing the "I bite" guy was Larry "Papa Hemingway" Cunningham. Just a guess.

Wilbur's General Store

A Small but Big Part of Little Compton, RI

In 2003, life was good for Karen Pritchard and her family. She had a job as a parish secretary, her husband worked in tech, the kids were thriving, and the family spent their summers in scenic, seaside Little Compton, Rhode Island.

That year, her husband, Michael, happened to glance at an ad in the local paper that read "General Store for Sale in Rhode Island." The Pritchards knew about the store, of course. Wilbur's General Store has been in town since 1893. It sits on the pretty town common, close to the United Congregational

Church, down from the library, close to the town hall and the few other stores in the small town. The Pritchards were also customers, having been in regularly to buy milk and other supplies for their summer cottage. But owning the store? That was another matter all together.

Still, Michael had always wanted to own his own business, and, frankly, says Karen, "He begged me."

Begging seems to have done the trick. Within a week, the papers were signed, and the entire family was on board with the decision. Now, more than a dozen years later, after several expansions, Wilbur's General Store is doing better than ever.

It turned out that despite having no previous retail experience, Karen had a real knack for running the store. Not that there wasn't some struggle at first.

"I remember those first few months, we just started going through the files," says Pritchard. "I asked questions—where do we get this, who are all of our vendors, who do we call for groceries?"

Photo by Art Donahue Photography

123

Karen Pritchard relied heavily on store manager Linda Gomes to show her the ropes. Gomes was Pritchard's first hire, and still manages the store. Pritchard's son and daughter worked the counter during summers, slowly figuring things out and making it their own. For the first few years, Karen Pritchard kept her secretarial job and traveled to Little Compton every week. Eventually, she gave up her "day job" in favor of focusing on the general store full-time. That focus undoubtedly helped.

"That first year we didn't know if we were going to make it," she remembers.

The Pritchards' first big step was to increase the quantity and quality of the food for sale at Wilbur's. Today, at the little store's meat counter, you can get meat ground to your specification, the steaks come directly from the same company that supplies high-end local restaurants, the turkey is roasted on the premises, and the famous store cheese, made right in Little Compton, sells more than 120 pounds a week.

As word of mouth spread, the Pritchards were able to expand the store. They now have a large gift and housewares section. Clothing is popular, too. For all that, from the outside, the little gray and white store with the green awning still seems, well, deceptively small. Karen Pritchard doesn't disagree.

"It looks about the size of a 7-11, but inside we have four rooms to the back and five rooms in another direction. You can find just about everything you want here—from a wedding gift to a hammer."

It hasn't all been clear sailing. A few years ago, a fire gutted the restaurant next door, threatening the Wilbur's building, also.

"It melted the siding," says Pritchard grimly. "This building was built in the 1850s; a fire is a very big deal."

But the hardy little store survived. Today, Wilbur's remains standing, a vital part of the tight-knit Little Compton community.

"People feel they can get what they need here; they don't have to drive two towns over," Pritchard says. "But it's also really a community center in a way, and I like that."

So does the community.

Harvard General Store

(HARVARD, MA)

Established in 1896

In New England, as elsewhere, "Harvard" has a certain Ivy League connotation. This is not that. In Massachusetts, Harvard is also a town 32 miles northwest of Cambridge. (And no, you don't "pahk" your "cah" there anymore than you do at the actual university's "yahd.")

History in Harvard is as varied and plentiful as the many apple orchards that dot the low, rolling hills of the town and this area of Worcester County in general. It was first settled in 1658 (only twenty-two years after Harvard University was founded) and

Photo by Ted Reinstein

incorporated as a town in 1732. Today the town common, still surrounded by proud seventeenth- and eighteenth-century homes, is as picturesque and quintessentially New England as it gets. It could be nowhere else. Across from the lower, southern corner of the common, at the intersection of the roads that lead to the present-day town of Bolton and the area once known as Still River, sits a handsome and distinctive three-story, flat-roofed, pale-blue-and-white wood building. There's been a building on the site with a long list of retail tenants going back 200 years. The store as it exists today—which represents the third building on the site—was established in 1896 but only became known as the "General Store" in 1978, when it was owned by Will and Joyce Garrick. As store owners go, the Garricks had a good run (twenty-six years), but reached the end of the line in 2004 and, without a buyer, closed the store. Three years went by. Sad ones for many in town.

"Sad, for sure," recalls Adam Horowitz. "The town had traditionally congregated at the store. When it was closed, it was as if the town center had simply dried up."

Unlike some in town, Horowitz and his wife, Lyn, were in a position to do something about it, although it didn't strike them that way at first. With a career in banking that frequently took him to London, Horowitz was headed back there in 2006, when the couple decided on a whim to look at the closed and darkened store.

"It was a mess, really, but we could see [that] the bones of the building were beautiful."

Nonetheless, there was an overseas trip to make and a plane to catch. But those beautiful bones beckoned.

"We're headed back to London, we took a look at it, we're already in the car headed to the airport," Horowitz says, hands raised, as Lyn shakes her head, smiling, recalling the crazy car ride. "We said, 'Look, if we don't make a decision, we'll get on the plane, and nothing will happen.' We turned around, came back, and made an offer."

Sitting outside the store at a picnic table on a warm August evening, the couple laughs now at the memory of almost impulsively deciding to buy a general store. But a year later, they were, in fact, the proud new owners of the Harvard General Store.

"Everyone knew that the key thing was to re-create the town's traditional gathering place," says Horowitz. "We said to the town, we're going to need help and cooperation, and the town was very helpful."

Photo by Ted Reinstein

Harvard had long been a "dry" town, but voters reconsidered and allowed a liquor license so the store could sell wine and beer. (Dealing with the sewer/septic issue was a heavier lift.)

The new store owners researched high-quality coffee and bread (They were mentored by legendary local coffee maven George Howell, who roasts his beans nearby in Acton, Massachusetts.) They hired local kids to work at the store and made new and creative use of the building's three stories. Lyn created an art gallery and gift shop on the second floor, and the third floor became home to a local newspaper, the *Harvard Press*. Townspeople were delighted that the store was open again. And the Horowitzes were happy to be making a go of it. But Adam Horowitz also learned a sobering lesson about being a storekeeper: People may love to know that you're there and you're open, but that doesn't necessarily mean you'll be seeing them regularly.

"Here's the paradox—no one wants to lose the store, but getting people to spend their day-to-day money, that's hard. It creates a sort of 'testing concept'—life without the store. Even in the 1930s, people would go to the supermarket in the next town, then, on their

Photo by Ted Reinstein

way back home here, they'd pop into the local store for the matches they forgot to pick up. Nothing new, it's always been frustrating."

In 2010, Adam Horowitz got an irresistible job offer in his field of banking and finance. It meant being based in London, and, sadly, he and Lyn made the move. For a while, they tried to keep things going with the store, but, as Lyn puts it, "It doesn't work to run a store from away." They needed to find a full-time manager. They found him right across the street. Literally.

Scott Heyward, a native of upstate New York, had worked for years in real estate development in D.C. In 1999, he moved to Harvard with his wife, who'd grown up in the Berkshires. They lived across the common from the store. For over ten years, they had front-row (or, in this case, living room) seats to watch the store's ups and downs.

"It was such a loss when it was closed, everyone felt it," recalls Heyward, who bought the store from the Horowitzs in 2012.

Sitting in the store with Heyward on a busy winter Saturday afternoon, it's clear he has given a lot of thought to a variety of ways to draw folks in. "We try to be the heart of Harvard, the center of the community," he says. The usual Saturday in-store farmers' market is going on, with two long tables filled with produce, breads, cheeses, and even fresh seafood.

"The farmers' market is going on two years now," says Heywood, waving to a patron. "I don't charge them; it's about them being here to get a good vibe of what the store's all about and to let them know we are all about local farms and supporting them."

Folks are grabbing lunch sandwiches from the busy café/kitchen counter area. Others are sitting at tables already eating or lingering over coffees.

"The store is an eclectic mix; I describe it as a three-legged stool—café, events space, and a grocery."

I might describe the Harvard General Store as having a few more legs, actually, at least as far as this historic building itself is concerned. The second floor today, above the store, is known as "Upstairs@the General." Community groups can use it for meetings and fundraisers, people rent it for parties and dinners, and bands regularly book it for live gigs. On the third and top floor, the *Harvard Press* ("Harvard's Independent Weekly Newspaper") soldiers on in its local journalistic mission. It doesn't bring any real revenue into the store itself, but Scott Heyward likes the fact that the newspaper calls the store home.

"It really goes to what this building is all about."

Then there's below the building. There is a bike shop in the store's basement. The building sits at a turn-around point for a major bike route out from Boston. On a summer Saturday morning, there might be more than seventy-five bikes in front of the store.

"Like I said, eclectic!" laughs Heyward.

All kidding aside, I ask him how things are going. After a long pause, he says, "We're five years in now. The first four years were difficult. We're beginning to get it now. It's a real learning curve, of your community, what works, what doesn't, what they want. Financially, it's about making it sustainable, that's what it has to be about—it's not going to be making anyone rich."

It does seem to be making locals happy, though. On this lazy winter afternoon, Harvard resident Ed Moussouris is lounging on a sofa in the middle of the big, second-floor space, coffee in hand, watching his two kids run about the big room with some other kids.

"It's a small town, there's not much else around, and it's a real community space. The food is excellent. I come in weekends with the kids," he says, deftly moving a full cup of apple juice on the floor out of the way of a careening toddler. "It's refreshing, it's a great gathering spot—hey, it would be very sad if it wasn't here."

Unlike Moussouris, who is quite a bit younger, Heyward indeed remembers when the store was closed. I ask him about the future. His answer seems to speak to not only about the Harvard General Store but about all such stores, everywhere, as an enduring American institution.

"I'm a very positive person," he says. "We still have some financial issues to overcome, but people need this, they want this. There are things going on in society and culture that make places like this important. We are definitely that 'third space.'"

ONE OF A KIND

There are almost fifty general stores profiled in this book. Each of them is distinct and different, ranging from when they started to where they're located to which of many particulars define them most individually today. In some ways, general stores are a bit like people—all have certain basic, common features, yet all have individual "personalities" that are entirely unique. Then there are the half-dozen stores that follow here. "Unique" doesn't begin to describe them. If all general stores have a personality, the following would have personalities described as "outsized." Looking for some lawn furniture, deer repellent, a wedding dress, and a new twelve-gauge? That's an easy, one-stop shop in Windsor, Maine. And nowhere else.

Hussey's

(WINDSOR, MAINE)

Established in 1923

The state of Maine is full of fun facts.

First, it's a big state. Not Texas big, but hey, all the other five New England states together could fit into Maine. One single county (Aroostook) is bigger than both Connecticut and Rhode Island combined. More fun facts about the Pine Tree State? It's the only state in America that borders only one other state (New Hampshire). Most Mainers would be happy to border no other state. But that would make Maine Hawaii.

"Flatlanders," or folks from "away," as Mainers are apt to say, often think first of the state's rugged and storied seacoast. A lobster sits right there on the state's license plate. (Further fun fact: The license plate lobster is red—in other words, dead, cooked. Live lobsters are dark green; why not add some melted butter to the license plate?) But the thousands of miles of coast are nothing compared to what's inland. Actually, what's inland is most of Maine. Ninety percent of the state is forested. (Final fun fact: That's the highest percentage of any American state.)

Central Maine is a land of rolling hills, woods, farms, all with a river running through it. The mighty Kennebec, which once powered lumber and textile mills, flows nearly 200 miles from Moosehead Lake to the Atlantic. The Kennebec Valley includes the state's capital, Augusta. As you drive east from there, away from the river, the land opens up and rolls and undulates through farms and fields like someone gently shaking out a great, green bed quilt. Ten miles east of Augusta, you'll find the rural town of Windsor. There, at the intersection of Routes 105 and 32, you'll see a tall sign (once featured on *Late Show with David Letterman*) that reads, "Guns, Wedding Gowns, Cold Beer."

Welcome to Hussey's.

"I was in college, and somebody said, 'Have you ever been to that crazy store in Maine?'" says Kristen Ballentyne. "And I realized she was talking about my family's store!"

 reference is placed above. The sign listing reads: CLOTHING, BRIDAL GO[WNS], GUNS, HUNTING SUPPLIES, FISHING, CAMPING GEAR, HARDWARE, PAINT, ELECTRICAL, PLUMBING, HOME & GARDEN, WOOD STOVES.

Photo by Ted Reinstein

Ballentyne (her married name) is a fourth-generation Hussey (pronounced, like the German, "HUZ-EE"). She grew up in Windsor, began working in the store when she was only eight, assigned, appropriately enough, to the toy department. Since then, and after going to college and getting married, she's done a bit of everything at the store, from customer service to the clothing department. If Hussey's, with its separate departments, doesn't sound like a smaller, more traditional general store, that's because it most emphatically isn't.

It is not a rural department store per se, but in other ways, it most certainly is. First, it is definitely not small. It's a big building that has three huge floors, from the basement up through the first floor to the second. By the large, central stairway in the middle of the first floor stands a 10-foot guidepost with arrows pointing to the different departments: Bridal Gowns, Guns, Hunting Supplies, Fishing, Camping Gear, Hardware, Paint, Electrical, Plumbing, Home & Garden, Wood Stoves.

Any questions?

"Honestly, the store is a little bit of everything," says Ballentyne. "As a general store, it's a pillar in the community, a tradition, and a social hub for people. Everybody knows you; locals buy groceries here."

Oh, right—there's a big grocery section, too. Needless to say, the store has grown quite a bit from its far more humble beginnings. Ironically, though, it was a grocery business that Harland Hussey essentially had in mind when he renovated a stable in 1923 and stocked it with simple provisions and some men's apparel. An industrious fellow, Hussey kept adding more and more lines of various merchandise, gradually outgrowing his cramped quarters. In 1954, the present building was opened. But growth has continued; today the store comprises over 30,000 square feet. Harland's son, Elwin, now ninety-three and born the year his father opened for business, is still a presence in the store.

"Oh, he loves to putter about," says Ballentyne of her grandfather. "He's very into old books; he'll add or rearrange things in the book nook or catalog old records."

Without doubt, the section of the store that surprises first-time visitors most is on the second floor, to the right of the fishing, hunting, and gun department. I mean, where else would you expect to find wedding gowns?

Ballentyne has heard it all before.

"Granted," she admits, "it does take some coaxing sometimes to buy a wedding dress at a general store."

To the initiated shopper, however, it's serious business finding what can be a bargain, even if it's a bit of a diamond in the rough. Or a gown amid the guns, as it were.

"People think they're second-hand," says Ballentyne, "but they're all new."

Her great-grandmother, back in the original store, had started a separate section for women who didn't want to drive to Augusta or all the way to Portland to find "special occasion" dresses. Eventually, that grew to include wedding gowns. When the new, larger store opened, the women's section, including wedding gowns, was alone on the second floor; the sporting goods were all on the first floor. Today, guns and gowns occupy the second floor together, and while both do a brisk business, the wedding gown section is a draw all by itself and attracts visitors from out of state.

Photo by Ted Reinstein

"It works well, actually," Ballentyne says of the unusual coexistence of cammo, ammo, and wedding wear.

"Often, ladies will look in the bridal section while their boyfriends are over in the sporting section. In fact, it often happens that a couple will buy a wedding gown and a gun at the same time."

Like you've never done that.

Ballentyne has. Sort of. On her own wedding day, she and her husband posed for a photograph beneath the "Guns, Wedding Gowns, Cold Beer" sign. Ballentyne looks resplendent in bridal white, while the happy couple clutches a six-pack and a shotgun.

"I had to get that picture," laughs Ballentyne. "I mean, I've heard the jokes about the sign forever."

Hussey's is New England's only general store where you can buy a wedding gown.

Just another fun fact from Maine.

From Homer's Death Mask to Hot Fudge

Let's face it: Guys have been known to acquire (and then resist ever getting rid of) some pretty strange things. When it comes to Chris Baker, we're not talking about your average velvet Elvis wall hanging or wagon-wheel coffee table.

"People laugh at me. My wife and children say, 'Why would you ever have something like Homer's death mask?' I bought it because I knew that someday there would be a literary person who would come in and absolutely die for Homer's death mask."

Any questions?

Actually, before Baker bought Homer's death mask, he bought an entire store in which said mask would ultimately find a home. But the store also has an attached emporium. This is not something you find every day. In fact, it is something you will find only in Mansfield, Massachusetts, where Old Country Store and Emporium has been a landmark on Otis Street for more than 180 years (making it arguably

Photo by Art Donahue Photography

the second-oldest continuously operating country store in America).

First, what it isn't: It isn't a grocery store/lunch counter kind of place where locals run in for a cup of coffee, quick chew of the daily fat with a familiar face while grabbing a stick of butter and a slice of Rhonda's rhubarb pie. It used to be that, back when it started out and Andrew Jackson was in the White House. It's changed over time, and today the store has all the feel of the real deal—all old, creaky wood floors and antique fixtures and a warmth and aged coziness that can't be denied and can be very, very welcoming when one steps away from the cold, cookie-cutter franchises in the strip malls, which, as it happens, are only a quarter mile away, making the refuge that is this country store—and the fact that it still endures—all the more satisfying.

"That's the funny thing. You pass the strip malls less than a mile away," Chris Baker says, shaking his head. "And then you take this funky little turn and here it is—you basically go back in time. And it's only a mile from those strip malls!"

So, what it is: It's a store filled to bursting with old-timey products and gadgets—one whole room alone is made up of wooden bins holding kitchen gadgets, some of which you may stand and stare at (as I did), and wonder, What the *#!@ is this thing? (The crazy thing is, you may then wonder how you've lived life without it.) There is a counter behind which old-fashioned homemade fudge of every flavor is made as customers watch. And there is a massive penny candy area. But attached to the store is a separate building and a barn that make up the "Emporium" part. Tough to describe. Tough to find anything similar that comes to mind, either. Suffice it to say there may be no other 200 year-old country store at which one can buy a box of fudge, a backscratcher, a hand-carved wooden mixing bowl, an area rug, a grandfather clock, a sofa, and a new but vintage dinette set.

Let's see—did we miss anything?

"We offer a little bit of everything for everybody," says Baker. "We have products ranging from 10 cents to $4,000. It sort of leads to the 'emporium' name—a large retail establishment with a wide array of merchandise."

There is no question about the wide array. Kids stare wide-eyed at the endless rows of candy. Adults of a certain age light up on seeing a product they remember from when they were kids. Music plays from a nickelodeon.

"I was walking into the barn the other day, and I heard a woman say, 'I'm in stinkin' heaven,'" laughs Baker. "So part of my job is to provide a little bit of heaven on earth. People can spend from an hour to four hours just roaming in here."

In his previous professional life, Baker likely never heard a customer say they were in "stinkin' heaven," but then international trade finance rarely seems to engender that sort of emotion. Chris and Lauryn Baker had taken a risk to move to Manhattan and make a go in that tough business. After twenty-five years of advancement and success, he'd reached his "own personal mountaintop," as Baker puts it, and was open to a change. The idea of returning to Massachusetts and buying the Country Store had sudden and strong appeal. With experience in risk-taking, the couple bought the store in 2010 from the Zecher family, who had been the owners for more than half a century.

"Like the Zechers did, there's no question I view myself as a caretaker," says Baker, standing amid a sea of kitchenware on a bright, early March morning in a mostly quiet store. "All of our associates, they realize this isn't just another job—you're part of the fabric, you're just as much a steward as I am. So we definitely want to keep the look and the feel the same, because it's like a well-worn pair of jeans: People are comfortable with it, they don't want dramatic changes. There's no sense in buying a place like this if you're going to make those types of changes."

So the institution that is the Old Country Store and Emporium marches on to the accompaniment of a creaking wooden floor, a vintage nickelodeon, and the evident and vocal delight of big kids and little kids lost in the dizzying array of Americana.

"I had the personal faith that the store had staying power," says Baker. "The community was supportive and always has been, because we couldn't keep the doors open without the folks who just love the store. I'm hoping in time to be proven not too crazy!"

Nah. Of course, there is the matter of that Homer death mask . . .

139

The Vermont Country Store

(WESTON, VT)

Established in 1946

"There are other ways to make a buck that are probably easier than running a general store or a retail business," smiles Cabot Orton. "But for us it's about going out and finding or creating things that connect us to the past, the tradition. We offer a chance to reconnect to a solid sense of principles, values, and the history we all find so compelling."

Sound somewhat big and lofty for a book about small and local general stores? Yes. But few families have given more thought to what general stores are genuinely all about than the Ortons. Not that theirs is a typical general store by any stretch, size, manner, or means, mind you. But then, you probably saw that coming. And if you've been to their store in Weston, Vermont, you've seen that for yourself.

In a way, the first thing you see about the Vermont Country Store is what you don't see. For a (very) little town (population 600), it's a very big store. But you won't see that from Main Street. The front actually looks like the very picture of the quaint, quintessential Vermont country store. Which makes sense, because it was one. But not in Weston.

Pull up a chair; this gets complicated.

The retail phenomenon that exists in Weston today actually had its start in the town of North Calais in 1897, when Melvin Teachout joined with his son-in-law, Gardner Lyman Orton, to open the Teachout-Orton Store. Orton moved to Athol, Massachusetts, in 1910 and opened a new store. His son, Vrest, moved on to New York and a career in writing and publishing, working with the legendary H.L. Mencken, then-editor of the *American Mercury* magazine. Vrest Orton, though, missed Vermont. He moved back, married in 1936, and began his own small publishing company, Countryman Press. After relocating to Washington, D.C., to work for the government during WWII, Vrest and his wife, Mildred, moved back once more to Vermont, this time for good. He had an inspiration for a new country store. Without the store.

Photo courtesy of The Vermont Country Store

"He felt, even in the 1940s, that the country store was disappearing in the United States," says his grandson, Cabot Orton. "So he wanted to re-create at least the sense of an old country store like the one his father and grandfather had run in the late nineteenth century. The irony was, Vrest Orton was about to tap nostalgia for the past by using a tool of the present: mail-order.

"In 1945, he created a fourteen-page pamphlet on the printing press in his garage—the store's first catalog," says Cabot Orton. "He and my grandmother bound it together on the dining room table, they mailed it to all of the people on their Christmas card list, and that's how we started the Vermont Country Store."

Vrest Orton carefully and methodically curated the products he would sell. They were largely handcrafts, local Vermont products and foods, all with an underlying purpose: usefulness.

"They couldn't just be gift items," says Orton of his grandfather. "They had to be practical and functional; that was very important to him. He felt that everything should have a purpose and be necessary."

Woven baskets, wooden utensils, cutting boards, jams—all were wrapped in plain brown paper, tied with twine, and dutifully mailed out each afternoon from the virtual "store."

The response was immediate and enthusiastic. Many customers wanted to come by and visit the store in person, but there was a slight problem—there wasn't actually a store. At least not in the physical sense. Vrest and Mildred managed a mailing list. You can't drop by and visit a mailing list.

"So many people who got the catalog were suddenly interested in seeing the actual store," says Orton. "And there wasn't one! So they had to scramble to create that physical experience."

In Vrest Orton's usual, methodical fashion, that's what they did. The building that he and Mildred purchased in Weston was built in 1827 and had been a longtime inn. (It also looked surprisingly similar to the original Teachout-Orton store back in North Calais.) But it soon became—or became once more—a very significant part of Weston, Vermont.

In fact, Vrest's re-creation became the first restored and operational rural general store in America (and today is on the National Register of Historic Places). In 1946, a year after mailing out their initial catalog, Vrest and Mildred opened the door of their actual, physical, brick-and-mortar Vermont Country Store. (Vrest Orton also had found time that year to become one of the three founding editors of *Vermont Life* magazine.)

"His intuition was that people were already nostalgic about old country stores they remembered," says Orton. "And they would really want to physically experience a piece of their childhood and relive the past, and that it would be an emotional and powerful experience."

Remember the famous line from the film *Field of Dreams* "If you build it, they will come"? It was true about creating a fictional baseball diamond and even more true about creating another—real-life— American institution equally steeped in sentiment and tradition.

Customers came from close by and far away to visit and browse the newly opened country store. Using his talent as a publicist, Vrest Orton succeeded in persuading the *Saturday Evening Post* (then

Photo courtesy of The Vermont Country Store

among the most widely read publications in America) to do a feature story about his and Mildred's unique and fledgling business. In 1952, "The Happy Storekeeper of the Green Mountains" story was published in the magazine, covering six pages with pictures. Nothing would ever be the same in Weston, Vermont. The happy storekeeper was also about to get very, very busy.

"It was lightning in a bottle for the Vermont Country Store," marvels Cabot Orton, shaking his head and smiling. "After that article, thousands of people wrote asking how they could visit the store and get that experience; it really, deeply captured people's imaginations."

On weekends and holidays, the little store was now often mobbed. By 1959, Vrest and Mildred were able to buy the house next door to the store, where they opened a restaurant called Bryant House. In 1968, business was booming enough to open a second store in Rockingham, Vermont.

In 1972, Lyman Orton, Mildred's and Vrest's son, became head of the company and brought the store fully into the modern era. Today, he and his three sons—Cabot, Gardner, and Eliot—run the business. While half their business is now done online, tens of millions of catalogs are still faithfully mailed out annually. The two store locations count over a million visitors a year, and the original Weston store is one of Vermont's most popular tourist attractions.

"It's something so many people enjoy and appreciate, and we're able to offer it to people from all over the country, all over the world—people come from England and Germany, they come from France, from Asia, to visit us here in rural Vermont and have a little bit of this experience."

In the spirit of nostalgia and pure whimsy, the Ortons have had fun bringing back products from earlier eras, sometimes updated. Are you old enough to have shampooed with Lemon Up?

"It's a product that disappeared from stores and supermarkets years ago," observes Orton, proudly brandishing a bottle. "We spent a lot of time and energy bringing this back, with the qualifier that it's actually improved because we replaced some ingredients that you might not want in your shampoo anymore—but it still has to be as evocative and smell as good as the original."

Today, the store in Weston is massive. One can walk through what feels like mazes of overflowing baskets and shelves of old-time products, penny candy, and traditional Vermont stalwarts like maple syrup, cheese, and handmade wooden toys, no doubt crafted by a transplanted, crunchy couple in down vests and plaid flannel shirts in a renovated hilltop barn. (Just kidding, the flannel's purely speculative.) There's a reason fall foliage tour buses pull up and disgorge thousands of visitors every year at the store, which, in turn, is enormous and expansive enough to handle such daily disgorgements. Visitors often amble and meander for hours, buying a knick knack here, a box of fudge there, inhaling the successive waves of nostalgia, carried along by it and by the sheer diversity of products and an inescapable sense of visual overload. (Back scratchers, bag balm, balsam—oh my.)

"Sure, it gets a little unwieldy and at times overwhelming, even to us!" concedes Cabot Orton with a grin. "But that's part of the experience and the charm—this eclectic, almost Byzantine assortment of unlikely items you'll never see anywhere else."

Clearly, it must be noted that the Vermont Country Store is not the same type of country/general store as many others in this book, or even in this chapter. In that sense, it is *truly* one of a kind. One doesn't dart into the VCS to buy a quart of milk or a dozen eggs. You don't swing by in the predawn, run in, motor running, for a coffee and a muffin to munch on in the car or truck, and locals don't drop by at midday to check their mail and maybe grab a grilled cheese. It's not that kind of general store. Its physical footprint and massive retail reach make it something else, entirely. (Indeed, in terms of simple square footage alone, a combination of multiple other stores in this book put together could all fit inside the Vermont Country Store.) What it provides instead is the *sense* of an old-time New England country or general store, with curated products and a carefully crafted environment that *evoke* the real thing.

"In a way, we are taking the idea of the country store, the ethos of the country store, and bringing it to the world," says Orton. "We think of a country store as more than just a physical place—it's an idea, it's a connection to the past, and, in a sense, it's a curatorial experience. That's what country store owners of the past would do—curate interesting products that people wanted or that would catch a customer's eye. We continue that tradition today."

That the Vermont Country Store represents an enormous retail success goes without saying. (At the time of this writing, negotiations were underway to open yet a third store in Vermont.) But the company will tell you that, however much it's grown far beyond it, its roots are still in that small, rural store way back in North Calais. Over time, Lyman Orton, having grown up in just such a community (Weston, Vermont), came to view such stores—and other similar, local institutions and traditions—as vital centers of small cities and towns across America, often where once-thriving main streets and downtowns are threatened and disappearing. In 1995, in an effort to help towns preserve some of these

elements, Lyman Orton (along with Noel Fritzinger) launched the Orton Family Foundation. Based in Burlington, Vermont, the nonprofit is funded by profits from the Vermont Country Store and awards grants to cities and towns to help them navigate growth and change or to hold onto or reclaim parts of their community that might otherwise be lost. (The foundation's core mission is "a barn-raising approach to community planning and development.")

Meanwhile, in Weston, droves of visitors continue to be drawn to the country store experience, delighting in its nostalgia and far-flung array of products, at the same time supporting what it represents in equally far-flung cities and towns elsewhere.

"We think this is why it's so evocative to people," says Cabot Orton. "It creates a sense of continuity in a world that's changing; we offer a chance to reconnect to a solid set of principles and values, and the history we all find so compelling."

And could Cabot's grandfather, Vrest, have ever foreseen what his little store grew into?

"I don't know if he ever could have foreseen it," Orton smiles, surveying the wide main storeroom in Weston. "But I think he'd be tickled to death, and he'd be pleased. And proud."

Dan & Whit's

"We're a general store that has a little bit of everything—kind of the predecessor to Walmart, that's the way we like to put it—everything old-fashioned and some of the modern conveniences."

It's tempting to let Dan Fraser's succinct description of his family's general store stand by itself and simply move on. But just as it's deceptive from the outside to get a full sense of the store itself, that description gives only a hint of what's really there. And if you've

Photo by Art Donahue Photography

never visited, well, what a shame to not get the full sense of things. Because there is nothing quite like Dan & Whit's.

The store sits in Norwich, Vermont, but is really more a part of New Hampshire's Upper Valley. Hanover, New Hampshire, sits just over the Connecticut River. It may technically be a state away, but a drive from the front of the stately Hanover Inn to the less-stately front of Dan & Whit's takes less than ten minutes. On the other hand, you couldn't adequately measure the contrast you've just experienced. For starters, you can't get gas in front of the Hanover Inn. Or quilted coveralls inside it.

Photo by Art Donahue Photography

"Yes, we have gasoline," says Fraser, a pleasant and soft-spoken thirty-something. He's just winding up to tick off the master list. "We have produce, we've got fresh meat, we've got wine, we've got groceries, we've got grain, we've got lots of hardware, we copy keys, we rent Rug Doctors, we sell urine for hunting season, really eclectic products that no one can find anymore."

Try finding pickled pigs feet, for instance, at your grocery store. (First aisle to the left as you enter Dan & Whit's. You're welcome.) It's interesting to watch first-time visitors look around. Eyes often widen. Or narrow. Expressions become quizzical.

"People are amazed," says Fraser. "It's kind of like taking a walk back in history. We don't like to change anything unless we have to. We like the old, wooden floors that creak. We have things here that are hundreds of years old that you'll find in a museum; we just use them every day. Former employees will come back after twenty years and say, 'Oh, my God—you still have that scale!'"

Yes, they do. Though it took me a few minutes to figure out what I was looking at. And yes, it is still very much in active service.

"How *old* is this?"

"Hm," says Fraser, bending down to look more closely. "Older than I can remember."

"But still works fine?"

"Sure, still inspected every year by the state of Vermont."

"So why change it?"

"Exactly."

Truthfully, little has changed at Dan & Whit's since Dan Fraser's grandfather, Dan, bought the place in 1955 with his high school friend and partner, Whit. It had changed little before that, too, when the two young men began working at the store in the 1930s, owned then by the Maral family. In the 1970s, Whit's family sold its half to the Frasers, and it's been entirely in Dan's family ever since.

Eventually, Dan, a teacher, came on board to help run the store full-time. Looking at a faded color photo of his grandfather from the sixties, it's easy to see a strong resemblance.

"He was the quiet one, my grandfather," Dan muses. "But had a great sense about things. One day he spotted a young boy steal an ice-cream sandwich and stick it in his pocket. My grandfather walked over and just got involved in a conversation with the boy for about twenty minutes till the ice cream melted down his pants. That was the last time he ever stole ice cream."

Not that you won't see plenty of (non-ice-cream-stealing) kids at the store. There's a big toy corner on the first floor, the perfect place for parents to plant the kids while they shop or browse, which, in a store full of fascinating, overly full nooks and crannies, can lead to its own problems.

"People wander around all the time, get lost in it, and that's what we like. But people have been known to come shopping with their kids, and the kids hang out in the toy corner, and the parents go home, then they call us and say, 'Is Billy still there? Because I forgot to bring him home.'"

Okay, that doesn't happen *that* often, Dan is quick to add. But easy to see here why it could. And the thing is, the front, main section of the store is not even the part in which

you're likely to get most lost. The part that is easily the most eye-opening thing about Dan and Whit's and, ironically, the thing most first-time visitors miss entirely is the legendary "back area." For all the creaking wooden charm, aisles of oddities, and assorted, still-active antiquities of the main store itself, there lies lurking just beyond it, a whole other world.

"Sometimes people live in town for six or eight months or even a year before they realize there is more out there," marvels Fraser. "And they ask for products, and we take them out there, and they are just amazed that it goes on and on."

It is, indeed, amazing. There's nothing to prepare you for it. There's a simple doorway just past the main store's meat counter. Once through it, you enter a literal labyrinth of five or so large, separate rooms packed with everything imaginable, from lawn and yard stuff, power equipment, rows and rows of huge grain sacks. Presumably, there is some sort of order to it all, but if you're like me, you will just find yourself being led along at a certain point just looking for where it all ends, because you think, Hmm, this building did not look big enough from the outside for what I am now walking through. It begins to seem star-tlingly possible that it doesn't end at all. That you have, in fact, just entered some other

Photo by Art Donahue Photography

dimension. That you walked into a lovely, if overstuffed, old-time general store, passed through a simple doorway, and are now stumbling zombie-like up and down endless rows of bird feeders, snow shovels, and kiddie pools in some latter-day HGTV episode of *The Twilight Zone.* Seriously, there are corn mazes out there that are easier to navigate through.

"When my grandfather ran the store, he expanded the business, so the footprint got larger and larger to the rear," Fraser explains. "But the footprint of the original old building in front stayed the same."

Oh. So that's it.

Dan has done some of his own expanding in terms of new stuff, such as wine tastings, which certainly would have struck his grandfather as an odd thing here for sure. But ironically, it's a perfect fit. Dan leads me down to the cavernous basement, the oldest part of the original building.

"Don't tell me," I say, looking around in the half-dark. "This now functions perfectly as . . ."

"A wine cellar," Dan chimes in proudly, gesturing at the floor-to-ceiling shelves of stored bottles. "The temperature down here, year-round, is perfect for wine."

"People expect to find a wine cellar at Dan and Whit's?"

"No, people are pretty surprised when I bring them down here."

There's also the surprise of the entire second floor of flannel, fleece, and every kind of warm and sturdy boot known to humankind. (There is likely no larger selection of hunting hats. One looked so warm and protective and just plain fetching, I bought it. I've never hunted.) The store's longtime slogan (not unique by any means) is "If we don't have it, you don't need it."

"Has anybody ever asked you for something that, lo and behold, you really don't have?" I wonder.

"Occasionally, it happens," admits Fraser. "Often it's something that is more modern technology that we really aren't up to speed on quite yet."

I mean, this is a store that is still using a nearly 200-year-old scale. Computers, Wi-Fi, and other daily digital mainstays may have to wait a bit before they're eased in here.

"We want to make sure a trend sticks before we invest in it," deadpans Fraser.

Hey, that old scale was cutting-edge once, too.

Of Special Note . . .

Clover Farm General Store and Country Village Yarn Shop/West Groton, MA

For starters, yes, that is the longest name of any general store you are likely to come across. Its owner, Janet Shea, is no less unique.

"This is where my son grew up, my daughter grew up, and I refuse to grow up."

Clearly, Shea is an original, and so is the Clover Farm General Store and Country Village Yarn Shop. The original Clover Farm Market was going through some hard times and, after struggling under two different owners, had closed in June 2012. Shea, who owned a longtime yarn shop right across the street, decided to do something crazy and save a beloved town landmark. With town approval, she merged the two businesses, and the result has brought a close-knit community (pun intended) even closer.

"We don't have a whole lot here in town, but what we do have we cherish, we absolutely cherish," says customer and West Groton resident Gail Chalmers. "Anyone else in town will tell you, the store is the hub of the town—if there's a wedding or a baby, we don't send out invitations here in West Groton; we just come down to the store to make sure everybody knows about it."

There's candy, sandwiches, coffee of course, and a selection of locally baked goods. The store does have Wi-Fi, but, shhh—they don't really want anyone to actually, you know, use it. Shea would much prefer people actually talk to each other, enjoy the quiet, slow down a bit. You certainly won't see any of the Monday afternoon and Thursday evening regulars texting. They're too busy knitting. Others might be borrowing from or lending a good read to the paperback book exchange. On a given visit, you could also walk in while a guitar lesson is going on. Have we missed anything?

It's a small store and a tidy one. Shea does it all, and the shelves may look a bit sparse from time to time. But what Shea is really selling is community. And in that, she is remarkably well stocked.

"I wanted this to stay a general store," she says. "I also believe I'm the only yarn shop in America with a beer and wine license."

Unique. Just like its owner.

THE NEW BREED

New England's general stores are nearly as old as the region itself. While a few have survived and endured with little outward change over the centuries, others have found the way to continued existence or rebirth only through reinvention. These stores have also relied on the inventiveness of new, younger owners who have found creative ways to blend the old and the new, essentially creating a new model for an old institution. They're pointing a path forward for how it's possible to do this. And stay in business.

Pittsfield Original General Store

(PITTSFIELD, VT)

Established in 1888

General store owners come from all backgrounds and have come to own or run their stores for many different reasons. For some, the store has been in their family for decades. Others have always loved the idea of owning a general store or have wanted to make a life change of some kind. Then there's Katie Stiles and Kevin Lasko. If you're going to endure competing in the brutal Spartan Races, you might as well come out of it with something more than a ribbon.

Photo by Cronin Hill Photography

The Spartan Beast is a series of grueling races run over courses bristling with tough and punishing obstacles such as barbed wire, climbing structures, deep mud puddles, and shooting flames ('cause, you know, merely *running* 26 miles isn't challenging enough). The race originated in Killington, Vermont, and Lasko and Stiles made trips from New York to compete there and around New England. Over time, they became friendly with one of the race's founders, Joe DeSena, who owned the longtime general store nearby to Killington in Pittsfield, Vermont, but was looking to sell it.

See where this is going?

"We were familiar with the area and had been into the store many times," says Stiles. "But I think what's a little bit different is that we're not from Vermont. The store has been here since 1888, and you can imagine there have been lots of people in this space operating it."

But no one quite like Stiles and Lasko.

They lived in New York City, where Stiles was a restaurant publicist, and Lasko was a *New York Times*–rated chef for the Manhattan restaurant Park Avenue. But in 2014, the couple uprooted, bought the Pittsfield Original General Store, and moved into the apartment above it.

"Before we took over the store, we visited many times and we did have an idea of what it should be and how the food should be and the service should be," Lasko says, as we stand in a corner of the store on a quiet, late March afternoon. "We just wanted to maybe bump it up a little bit and use better quality food and use the really good-quality products that are available here."

The couple looks about the store; Stiles waves to a customer grabbing a coffee.

"It really is sort of the quintessential general store." She smiles, as if admiring something dear but still new. "We wanted to create a sense of community, a sense of place, but also really highlight some of the really cool stuff going on in Vermont and cool products that are available here."

So far, they've done that. And, as importantly, they haven't done some other things, like dramatically change what is an old-time general store long familiar to locals.

"Pittsfield is a unique place, and there are people here who've been here for many, many generations," says Stiles. "And we really want to make them happy and do the right thing here. So we listen to them, listen to what they're interested in."

The store's original wide, wooden floor planks still bend, dip, and creak in sections. The wood is warm, authentic, and inviting. There are shelves of all the basics and, in the back corner, a children's book nook. A freezer near the front door is full, naturally, of Ben & Jerry's ice cream. Beer and wine fill the long freezer lining one wall of the main room. Vermont-made products (from maple syrup and cheese, to granola and yo-yos) are every-where, and the deli counter is busy all day and into the early evening.

"We're on Route 100 (a scenic Vermont road that serves many ski areas), so we attract people who are here but also people who are driving through," Stiles points out. "So we want to do stuff that is appealing to both groups and make sure we're doing stuff that's interesting to both."

What they did after only about a year in Pittsfield was a bit more outside the box.

Literally.

"I ran a large restaurant in New York, with no interaction with guests," says Lasko. "But I was also doing a ton of smaller dinner parties at people's houses, and it was great because everyone was talking and interacting. And we were like, how can we turn that experience into a restaurant?"

The answer came later, and well north of those Manhattan dinner parties. DeSeno, from whom Stiles and Lasko bought the store, also owned a nearby inn and wedding venue. The couple made a condition of the sale that they would cater the weddings and open a small restaurant on the store's property. In February 2015, only a year after pur-chasing and reopening the store itself, Stiles and Lasko opened the Back Room.

As a venue, it's a bit hard to describe, but "restaurant" doesn't quite do it. It's an entire separate, small, one-room building behind the general store. Large, heavy wooden doors open into it; some have described it as like entering a speakeasy. It's open only on week-ends, only one seating nightly, and seats only twenty at two long communal tables.

Chef Kevin presides at a counter in front of it all, a sort of very open kitchen, preparing tasting menus, while Stiles mixes esoteric drinks and wines paired with the fresh offerings of the night. Very fresh.

"All these restaurants in New York are doing farm-to-table and it's very interesting," says Stiles. "This is *truly* farm-to-table—here, we literally go across the street and pick up our stuff from the farmer! We talk to the farmers about what cuts of meat Kevin wants, and they go and slaughter it and package it and it's specifically brought to us."

It's different, that's for sure. Deliciously so.

"Everybody's coming for a little bit of adventure," Lasko observes. "I mean, we're asking a lot of our guests—they come at a set time, they eat a set menu, they don't know what it's going to be, and they're sitting with strangers. And so they're in it for an experience, they're in it for something new, and they're down for doing whatever we're trying that night."

On a chilly, early spring night, it certainly feels like people are happily going with the flow. It's a warm and cozy gathering; folks introduce themselves and chat before dinner,

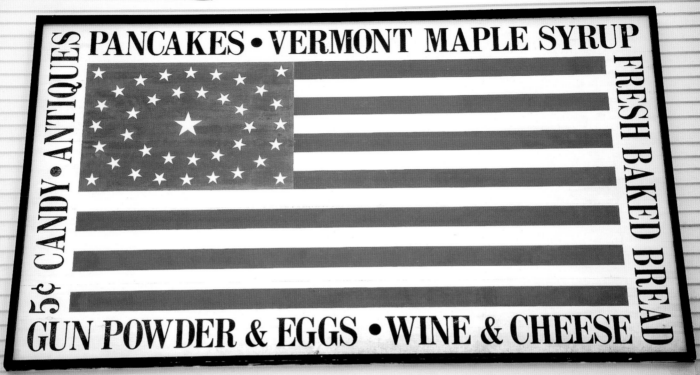

PANCAKES • VERMONT MAPLE SYRUP

5¢ CANDY • ANTIQUES

FRESH BAKED BREAD

GUN POWDER & EGGS • WINE & CHEESE

Photo by Cronin Hill Photography

as they would at an intimate dinner party. (Indeed, the *New York Times* described the Back Room as an experience "that feels like New England's coolest dinner party.") Guests mingle first for a cocktail hour, feeling free to ask the chef about what he's preparing, as he prepares it. It's followed by a three-course menu. It's homey. Friends are made.

"The best thing is when people return to the Back Room with people they met the first time," laughs Lasko. "They never knew each other—and they'll come back together to have dinner!"

It's what Stiles and Lasko had in mind back in Manhattan when they dreamt of opening something like this. They just couldn't have predicted that there'd be a general store attached to it. But the Back Room and the general store in front now seem to complement each other.

"Definitely," says Stiles. "We do a smoked maple butter, and people will have it and go, 'This is fantastic!' and we say, 'Oh, we have that in the store!' We have so many customers in the Back Room who'll say they've never been in the store, and then we'll see them here the next morning, browsing, and they're like, 'This is great!'"

The Pittsfield Original General Store is a unique hybrid for sure. But nowadays, it may take just such experimenting and creativity for a lot of stores to survive. It isn't enough to love a familiar place on the corner. A store is still a business, not a monument. Communities and their demographics change. It's about finding a niche that works where you are. Whether it's Pittsfield, Vermont, or Monterey, Massachusetts.

"Even with community support, they do need to be successful," points out Paul Bruhn, executive director of the Preservation Trust of Vermont. "You have to find what works in your community."

It's what Kevin Lasko and Katie Stiles are finding.

"I think there's definitely a changing face to the general store," says Stiles.

Lasko agrees. "They have to remodel themselves to the times and what the demands are. But they are still a unique thing because they are a utility for everyone. I mean, if you're out to get bread, you need a place that's not 30 miles away. But at the same time, it can be something that's new and interesting and that will keep them coming back for more than just bread."

So the couple from the big city is making a good and steady go of it in the mountains of southern Vermont: running an old general store with new twists and a restaurant out back that is all about new twists mixed with some old-time qualities, like talking to your neighbor.

"It's a lot more work than we thought it would be, that's for sure," says Lasko.

Tougher than running a Spartan Beast race through the mud and under barbed wire?

Big laughs all around, but no denial.

Sheepscot General at Uncas Farms

(WHITEFIELD, ME)

Established in 2015

As counties go, Maine's Lincoln County is an interesting one. For one thing, it has shrunk over the years. A lot. While today it primarily hugs a stretch of south coastal Maine, at its founding in 1760, it accounted for three-fifths of the state's total land area and extended all the way north ("Downeast," in Mainer parlance) to Nova Scotia. Today, nearly a third of the county's 700 square miles is water, and many of its best-known communities are synonymous with maritime Maine: Boothbay, Damariscotta, Monhegan Island. But Lincoln County also extends north from the coast, inching into lower central Maine, just south of

Photo by Ted Reinstein

the state's capital at Augusta. As you make the drive away from the coast, the hills become wider and more rolling. The road winds by woods that suddenly open up to long, stretching acres of farmland. Some of the farms are really old, scratched out of the rocks and trees over centuries, hardy as the history they entail. In the mornings in warmer months, the closeness to the coast often creates ghostly, low-hanging fog banks over the fields. Old, wooden barns seem to poke out of the mist like faded, red apparitions. In the midst of this uniquely Maine landscape, along a long straight stretch of Maine Route 26, you'll find the small town of Whitefield. And down Townhouse Road, you'll find Uncas Farms where you'll also find, however unexpectedly, a most unusual general store.

Photo by Ted Reinstein

Uncas is a Forever Farm, a designation for Maine farm properties that have been protected and preserved through agricultural conservation easements. It's partly owned by Daniel Ridgell, who divided his operations between the cattle part and the smaller five acres that Ben Marcus and Taryn Hammer manage (and now own), which includes the store.

"Dan had been looking for tenants; nothing had worked. We were the first people to approach him," explains Marcus as we sit just outside the store at a picnic table on a warm August afternoon. He and Hammer are young, late twenties or early thirties, and met at the agricultural program at Washington State University. Hammer grew up in Wisconsin; Marcus grew up in Whitefield, just down the road from Uncas Farms. When he was a kid, what is now the general store was a natural foods store. After college, the two came to Maine with the intent to farm somewhere. They gave it their first shot on Marcus's family's land, planting fruit trees.

"We kept driving by the Uncas Farm place and it was the biggest farmland around," recalls Hammer. "But it was all going to weeds."

Photo courtesy of Sheepscot General

They approached Ridgell and began renting and farming the land in 2011. Marcus and Hammer married in 2013 and two years later marked another big transition: They bought their share of the farm. Although all the couple wanted to do was farm, Ridgell added a stipulation: They had to also reopen the defunct store on the property. As an inducement, he included a $5,000 loan to help reopen it. All good, except for the small fact that Marcus and Hammer had no real interest in running a store or any retail experience whatsoever.

Oh, to be young. They gamely jumped in.

"The first thing we did was take down the old 'Natural Foods' sign," laughs Hammer. "We knew we wanted to attract a more diverse group."

The second thing they had to do was actually fill the store with products. And then, hopefully, customers.

Photo courtesy of Sheepscot General

"Actually, when we opened the store, we had almost nothing in it," Hammer laughs. "So we decided to just put stuff in it that we like—that way, if it didn't work out, we figured we'd just eat it all ourselves!"

But a funny thing happened: it worked out.

"We were shocked that people came out and bought stuff!" Hammer exclaims.

"Yeah," Marcus interjects, "but it helps that we didn't pay ourselves, either."

Aside from the shock that people actually dropped into the store and bought stuff, the other realization for the couple was that it wasn't just a loaf of bread, a carton of milk, or a crate of eggs that seemed to draw people in. It was something else. Something that had been missing.

"There's nowhere else in town to sit down and have a cup of coffee," Hammer says. "That's the biggest thing we realized when we first opened—all these people live in the same town but had no common place to run into each other."

Now that folks were running into each other at the store and tarrying over their groceries and produce, Hammer and Marcus realized they needed to offer more than the bare necessities. By merely opening, they had filled an empty space (figuratively and literally) in town. Now they began filling other empty spaces. There was no town library in Whitefield, so they created a small lending library at the store. They also realized within the first year that they needed to have prepared food at the store.

"We had chefs approach us about doing farm-to-table," says Hammer, "but we wanted to keep it real simple and connect directly with our people."

They began baking their own bread, over 100 loaves a week, and donating whatever was left to a local food bank. Their deli counter offers soups and sandwiches, and they do a Friday Pizza Night.

"Our vision is kind of a combination farm, store, and café," says Hammer.

The vision certainly seems to have caught on with the community. After all, ROMEO bought in.

"Retired Old Men Eating Out," Hammer laughs. "Seriously, that's when we knew we were really connecting. The old town guys were coming in and hanging out. We didn't just want old hippies coming in."

There's nothing wrong with old hippies, mind you. But clearly, it's a diverse and eclectic crowd that frequents Sheepscot General. On this particular afternoon, kids are scurrying around waiting on parents who are picking up groceries. A middle-aged man works on a laptop at a café table.

"Hey, they have Wi-Fi and I take full advantage!" laughs David Dechlefs, a Connecticut resident who's been summering in the area for years. "They ask how my kids are, local people come in, we love being here for Pizza Night—it really tries to be a community place."

Because Dechlefs goes back far enough here to remember when the place was a natural foods store, I can't resist asking.

"Older hippies still feel comfortable here?"

"Lots of old hippies," he laughs. "But a lot of young hippies, too!"

The former milking barn attached to the store has been turned into a large community room. There are kids' dance classes, yoga classes, men's and women's groups all using the room, as well as lectures offered there. And Hammer and Marcus, who had planned to be farmers not store owners, are doing some farming, too.

"We farm now to support the store," says Marcus.

In 2015, they were Maine's only location for pick-your-own organic strawberries. They also grow produce, do maple-sugaring, and take care of two apple orchards.

"And we're well networked with other local farmers in the area for chicken, meat, and eggs," says Hammer.

Do they miss farming full-time the way they had once dreamed of?

Photo courtesy of Sheepscot General

"Sure," Hammer concedes. "I miss it a bit."

"Actually," counters Marcus, "I have to say, I'm kind of grateful for this now. I see other farmers racing around, having to hit all the farmers' markets; now I see us as kind of linking all these people together."

So the farmers-turned-general-store-owners continue to grow their own unique hybrid of farm and store, harvesting something good for them and good for their community in what has been a kind of bumper crop all its own.

"We're making it," says Marcus. "We're paying ourselves—not minimum wage yet, but it's a salary—we have a staff now, and we're not going anywhere."

They both wave and exchange greetings with an older regular who's pulled in.

"Ultimately, it's pretty simple," says Hammer. "If the community supports it, it'll work; if not, it won't."

No one in Whitefield would want to bet the farm on anything. But they sure want the Sheepscot store to be there for a good, long time. Old hippies and all.

Monterey General Store

(MONTEREY, MA)
Established in 2012

Tucked amid the rolling, rounded, low peaks of the Berkshires, the southwest corner of Massachusetts has always seemed a bit of a set-apart and enchanting place to me. Just the names of some area landmarks themselves seem dusted with whimsy: October Mountain, Jacob's Pillow, Beartown State Forest.

But forests and mountains can't close. Alas, other landmarks can, such as the Monterey General Store. But first, some background.

Photo by Art Donahue Photography

There is a penchant for culture, creativity, and independence in these hills. Nonconformists have always fit in here, so it's no surprise that, in summer, the tiny town of Becket has long attracted dancers. Music has long had a summer home at Tanglewood. Similarly, it also makes perfect sense that, in the film *Alice's Restaurant,* Arlo Guthrie ran afoul of the law in Stockbridge, or that former Yankees pitcher and baseball iconoclast Jim Bouton (author of the once-scandalous *Ball Four*) lives nearby in South Egremont. You can feel very free to be you and me in the Berkshires. It's sort of the Bay State's answer to Vermont.

The town of Monterey is a classic Berkshire hill town. It has a year-round population of just under 1,000, though it swells to more than twice that in summer. (Such is the lure of the cool woods and hills, and such is the proximity to Manhattan.) There's a couple of lovely lakes, a post office, a charming little library, and a lot of cool people doing whatever they want to be doing off on their cool, wooded plots of land. At the town's "center" (defined essentially by the junction of Tyringham Road and Route 23 and not much else), a handsome, sturdy-looking, two-story wood building has stood for over two centuries. For much of that time, it housed a general store that was both a vital commercial link and an equally vital community gathering place for generations of Monteruvians (their term,

not mine). For an unfortunate period of time after 2011, though, the store's vitals were, well, flat. It had expired. Closed.

But it's funny sometimes how two people find each other. Or, in this case, one person and a building.

"First and foremost, I fell in love with the building itself, even though it was in difficult shape. I loved how it sat on the little brook that runs through town," explains Scott Cole. "The funny thing is, I had come close to buying it way back when but walked away."

But timing is everything, and in 2012, Cole and the little building on the brook were finally ready for each other.

"It was good timing," Cole agrees. "I had some friends here in Monterey. At my café in West Stockbridge, we had sold provisions, we had a bakery, we were sort of a mini-version of a store, but I wanted to expand on all those notions."

For almost twenty years, Cole had owned and run the Caffe Pomo D'oro in West Stockbridge, Massachusetts. But with the Monterey store back on the market, he saw an opportunity to create something new tied in with something old.

"We live in such a different age now. People have gotten away from doing local shopping; they think nothing of driving twenty minutes or more to the grocery store. But there's also been a real resurgence of interest in local makers, whether they are goods or foods, to return to something more localized, and not just mass market–produced."

But first Cole had to get an old building with a defunct store into shape to draw new customers. He spent the early part of 2012 hiring people to help him realize his vision, starting with the decidedly nonromantic work of renovating a very worn and weary building.

"I wanted it to have the feeling of an old country store," says Cole. "Unfortunately, over the years, little had been done to enhance the character of the building. I spent months stripping away the layers of bad decisions to bring it back to its core and then to add an interesting mix of things."

That mix of things was finally unveiled late in the summer of 2012, when all the stripping away and starting fresh yielded a new and reopened Monterey General Store to a community that embraced it with an ardor that showed nothing if not how much they had missed it. Four years after the reopening, there is still a palpable delight among the regular customers that the store is there and operating once again.

"What's not to love? It's like an old-time general store," exclaims Lisa Henriques, a Monterey resident. "I come in, and I forgot my money—I get what I want and come back later and pay. Where can you do that? You're among friends here."

The store does indeed seem in some ways like an old-time general store. But it also seems oddly contemporary at the same time. Dark wooden shelves showcase upscale and imported food products, and a kitchen hums busily off to one side behind a counter under a huge menu board, but the wood floor lacks only fresh sawdust in its old-timey feel of age and authenticity. On a raised level, there are small tables and chairs where friends meet up and sip coffee and eat. Through a back door, there's a deck with more tables overlooking the brook and a small duck pond—a very popular spot to sit and linger in warmer months.

"The back deck is amazing; it's such a bucolic place to have breakfast," says regular Charlie Ferris, an attorney who's lived in Monterey since 1984. "It might appeal to weekenders more now than in the old days, but Scott is a great baker and locals support it, especially all the local produce he uses."

Cole walks the walk when it comes to using locally sourced food at his store. He's one of the founders of Berkshire Grown, a regional group that supports and promotes local agriculture.

"It all revolves around a network of local farmers that I've worked with for the last twenty-five years, so there is a real community of people who take great care in the food they grow or the animals they raise."

Cole's baking has created something of a cult following. Pies, tarts, croissants, scones, breads; it's not unusual for people to ask if pies can be shipped (they can). But that's the part that Cole was used to at his former place in Stockbridge. It's the new, "general" part of the store that he's still getting adjusted to.

"This is harder for a number of reasons. There are so many little details that have to be dealt with every single day: making sure the newspapers are here and put together, making sure the products are fresh and what people want."

Cole is steadily testing out what people want, what they might respond to. He's doing music nights in winter and early spring, offering a dinner menu on certain nights, and showcasing the work of local artists.

On this day, a late summer Sunday afternoon, people are sitting on the back deck, enjoying the fading sun and the tasty food. I strike up a conversation with Alexis Kennedy, a mom of young twin boys who are exploring the deck more than their lunch. Kennedy's dad grew up in Monterey, her husband grew up next door in Tyringham.

"Easier to find a table here in November?" I ask.

"Sure, it's less touristy in non-summer," she shrugs, "but that's the double-edged sword, right? We love it here, it feels like home, it's beautiful."

Her husband, Chris, chimes in, waving at his plate.

"And not the usual fare you'd expect at a general store—caprese salad!"

Photo by Art Donahue Photography

Old and new.

"It's a real mix, and really, it's a lifeline sometimes," says Melissa Mishcon of Monterey. "This is a small town, and not everyone has Wi-Fi, so the store becomes kind of a palazzo of the neighborhood. Sometimes you see people on the back deck long after the store is closed."

"We have a tiny library, we have a church," says Cole. "This general store really is a place where people count on interacting with their neighbors, it really is."

Scott Cole's general store doesn't look exactly like the one whose place it took. But then, the twenty-first century isn't the eighteenth.

"But there is still such a place for it, and I think what's important and exciting about it is that people have taken the concept of a general store and sort of deconstructed it and reinterpreted it in a way that suits them," observes Cole. "One of the reasons people respond even to just the words 'general store' is that they conjure a specific idea of old timey everything, and I do think people respond to being able to have a connection to a community, where things were made by someone who they can meet and be part of the process, in a way. It's why farmers' markets are proliferating, and I think that happens in a place like this."

Like it used to be, it is once more; but now it has Wi-Fi, wine pairings, and caprese salad.

Hope Down East

Hope General Store in Hope, Maine, occupies a historic building built in 1832. But it had been closed for six years when Andrew Stewart first peered into its basement in 2005.

"There was mold everywhere, and there was what seemed like sixty years' worth of garbage down there," said Stewart.

Undaunted, Stewart decided the 173-year-old store was exactly the kind of project he had been looking for. "I needed the general store and the general store needed me."

Never mind that there wasn't much of a store left because the building had become more of a workshop than anything else. The apartment upstairs, where Stewart planned to live, didn't show much promise either. And never mind that Stewart had never run a general store before. Or any store.

Hope, Maine, is a town of less than 2,000 people sitting a bit inland and just to the west of well-known coastal towns like Camden and Rockport. Stewart found himself in this unlikely place after floating from previous stays in London, Seattle, Botswana, and a few other stops along the way. (Just "seeing the world," as he puts it.)

Despite his complete lack of retail experience, Stewart didn't lack for ideas. There had been no grocery store in Hope for years. In addition, there was really no place for locals to meet up and get together. Stewart started renovations and started reaching out.

"People were really excited. In fact, they were so excited that they continually stopped in to chat during the renovations, which added quite a bit of time to the project. I couldn't get anything done."

For all his world traveling, it seemed like the town of Hope had been waiting for Stewart. From the beginning, he wanted to bring people into the store not just to shop but to spend time with their neighbors. He sold fishing licenses, soccer balls, tofu, and beef jerky. He put in a few tables. Opened a deli. He also stocked the store with 140 different kinds of craft beer, which was a big draw from the beginning and has remained so ever since.

Hope may be a small town, but it seems to like a lot of choices.

"I remember we had organic ketchup, Heinz ketchup, and a cheap ketchup. That's because Hope is a unique kind of town, it has a wide variety of demographics—not wide enough to support a big order of curry paste, though. That never sold particularly well," laughs Stewart.

And along the learning curve, Stewart learned how to run a business.

"The deli was the focal point, everything else was secondary. I mean, I wasn't going to survive selling a can of peas for $1.19 with a 30-cent profit."

The store did survive and thrive, each year doing better than the one before.

Perhaps more important than simply allowing residents to get groceries locally again, the opening of the Hope General Store seemed to kick-start a new community spirit. There was a triathlon, a children's festival, a jazz festival, and a winter festival, among other community events, all supported in one way or another by the Hope General Store. Stewart joined the volunteer firefighters and also served on several town boards. One day, Stewart overheard someone say, "Gee, I never knew Hope was so hip." Days later, bumper stickers were being sold in the store that read "Hope Is Hip."

Over seven years as the store's owner, Stewart hired local college and high-school kids to work behind the counter. He met and married his wife, they had two children, and Stewart decided he needed to move on. He sold the store in 2013 and now owns a pub called the Drouthy Bear in Camden, a few miles away.

Fortunately for Hope, its general store is still open. It is currently run by one of Stewart's first employees.

"Renee walked in the first day we opened, and I asked her, "Do you know how to make pizzas? Because I don't, and we have lots of orders."

Renee Kimball stayed and never left. The store is still selling sandwiches, soccer balls, and staples, but it's the friendship and the rediscovered sense of community that comes with it that makes folks in Hope happiest. And hip.

Photo by Jamie Bloomquist Photography

West Townshend Country Store

Established in 2011

As we've seen, sometimes it takes a village to save a store. Sometimes it also takes some pizza. But that comes later in this story.

West Townshend (and Townshend, five miles to the southeast) in south central Vermont is named for someone who was not a particularly popular person in early American history. Charles Townshend was Britain's Chancellor of the Exchequer when, in 1767, Parliament passed the infamous acts bearing his name. The acts were directed at the

Photo by Robert DuGrenier

rebellious American colonies, imposing taxes on a variety of goods and products— including tea. How'd that work out for you, Mr. Townshend?

Early settlers in this part of Vermont were mostly farmers, never an easy task in the Green Mountain State's rock-studded hills. By the nineteenth century, manufacturing and the advent of tourism improved things in both West Townshend and all of Windham County. In the early 1960s, the construction of the Townshend Dam on the West River flooded a large area of land. This was good for generating power, but bad for preserving parts of a town slated to become a lake. (At least West Townshend survived intact as a town on the map. In 1938, when work began on the creation of the Quabbin Reservoir in central Massachusetts, four entire towns were disincorporated, depopulated, flooded, and lost beneath the rising water.)

But along with the survival of the town itself, a physical symbol of the town's enduring history—in fact, the last commercial building standing in town—also survived: the West Townshend Country Store. Constructed in 1848, it served as a general store for the original owners for sixteen years, a place for local farmers to trade and barter for goods and produce, as well as a place in which to gather around the store's stove and trade hot, local gossip.

Over the next 150 years, the store, like many others, went through a succession of owners. But it was a tough environment, standing by itself on State Route 30. By 2000, the store itself was vacant; only the local post office still occupied the historic but hollowed-out building. In 2001, a fire heavily damaged part of the building. Ahead, clearly, lay demolition.

"The person who owned the building was set to close it and shut down the post office," recalls Robert DuGrenier. "And a bunch of us got together and said, you know, if we lose this little community center here, we'll never see our neighbors, we'll never come down off the hill, and we'll lose a sense of place that a lot of us are so proud of and fond of."

DuGrenier, a West Townshend glassblower, artist, and farmer, joined with others to hold onto their little, local post office. They formed the nonprofit West River Community Project. In 2012, with help from the Preservation Trust of Vermont and an angel investor, the new group was able to secure a twenty-year lease for the building. The West

Townshend Country Store would live on after all. Its venerable walls, though, would soon house more than its original owners could ever have imagined.

The building was extensively renovated, repainted, and repurposed in some new and very different ways. In the basement, a commercial-quality community kitchen was installed to serve not only a café upstairs, but other community uses as well, from cooking classes to local bakers to helping incubate and launch local businesses using local products. On the ground floor, where the store itself once was, a café now greets visitors with coffee, baked goods, soups and sandwiches, and local products such as fresh-baked bread, cheese, honey, and maple syrup. The walls are covered with local artists' works. A nice touch is that not only is there free Wi-Fi, but there's a free community computer for use in the café. On the second floor is a thrift store that offers second-hand clothes and shoes. This is not a small thing for some folks in this area.

"You can come here and, like my grandson who is growing, for a dollar I can get him some really nice clothes," an amiable grandfather exclaims. "I come here all the time; sometimes I come here almost every day just to check out what's new. And okay, I come to chitchat, too!"

As the interior of the store was being renovated in 2012, neighbors also began construction of a wood-fired, earthen oven outside. Now, on Fridays, the store holds a weekly Pizza Night where locals can make their own pizza, with everything locally sourced, from the toppings to the wood under the fire to the live music.

"Building the community oven was one of the first steps that really unified the community," says DuGrenier. "You know, fire, food, music—it's a magic combination."

There is also a community art gallery and an event space for use by local performers. A small lending library encourages visitors to take a book and leave a book.

But with all these diverse elements under one roof, perhaps what's most interesting today about the West Townshend Country Store is what's not there. There are no small aisles of packaged products, no shelves of canned goods or boxes of cereal. In other words, no "store" in the way we commonly think of a country store. Instead, what they have achieved is a remarkable distillation of a good country store's most essential qualities: filling the need of a specific community and creating a place for that community to gather, have a bite, and share a conversation with a neighbor.

"We don't have the groceries, but we do have a smiling face who knows your name," says DuGrenier. "And if they don't, they will find out before you leave!"

DuGrenier, now the president of the WRCP nonprofit, doesn't take knowing his neighbors lightly.

"I moved from New York City twenty years ago and had more people in my high-rise building than we have in this whole town. I knew one person in that building. Here, there are 200 people in the village, and I know everyone. That's fantastic!"

So the West Townshend Country Store has survived and has been able to chart a new course. It is not everything it once was, but it is also many things it never was, all because a small community would not let the last remaining link to their shared past be washed away like so much surplus land or disposable property. They saved it, and they created something new.

"It's the passion that I've put into it and a lot of other board members have put into the place that has transformed it into a place we love now," says DuGrenier, "We really wanted to have a place that was a village, and this really accomplished that."

And some of the old still remains. The post office that inspired the original efforts to save the building? Still there, out behind the café. That would be West Townshend, VT, zip code 05359.

Postscript

For all the variety of stories in the foregoing chapters, for all the diversity in the kinds of stores themselves out there, there is one inescapable, unarguable truth that ties them all together. Despite their collective long sweep of history, longevity was never assured for any of them. Neither is continued survival. For general stores, survival has always been, and remains, a constant challenge. Consider just one legendary general store and how circumstances changed just in the matter of months between our visit and writing the very end of this book.

"The margins are *so* thin," sighed Lyssa Papasian, when we spoke on the front porch of Vermont's Putney General Store on a sunny afternoon in October 2016. "The store is still hanging by a thread."

Since then, the thread broke. The Putney store (Chapter 4/Unsinkables) is the ultimate survivor. It has endured more crushing setbacks in its 200-year history than any other store of which we know. And it has consistently managed to recover and rebound. In addition to weathering all the same national travails (wars, depression, recessions) that its counterparts have, the Putney store has also been ablaze. Twice. The second time (only a year after the first), it burned to the ground, leaving nothing of its long and colorful history but smoke and ashes. But, like the mythical phoenix, the store rebuilt and reopened. Twice. As cursed as its history might seem, however, the store has also been abundantly blessed with a community that has long been loyal, supportive, and doggedly determined to hold onto its general store. But there are limits. After all the goodwill, someone has to actually *operate* the store daily. In recent years, the building itself has been owned by the Putney Historical Society, which had found a good fit for a viable store owner in a pharmacist who was able to both run the store on the first floor and his pharmacy on the second. It worked well for years. But late in 2016, after an illness, the store owner died, and his family was not interested in continuing to operate the store. On December 31, 2016, Putney General Store closed its doors. Happy New Year.

"As the building owner, our goals are to as quickly as possible reorganize and reopen the store under a new owner/operator-tenant, or on an interim basis under our ownership and management until a new tenant can be found," Papazian updated us in an e-mail. "We don't know yet how long this may take."

Continued survival is not assured.

The thing is, despite being a beloved anchor in a community, general stores still can—and do—fail for any number of reasons. Each year in New England, a handful continue to close. Part of the problem is mythology. Not in the "Putney store-as-phoenix" sense, but in terms of the popular conception of a general store. In small towns across New England, many stores have been around as long (or longer) as other iconic, local institutions, like churches and libraries. Over time, neighbors often come to regard the local general store—often within a stone's throw of the church or library—in the same way, as an institution that is "just there," a familiar, permanent presence that centuries have seamlessly woven into the town's historical tapestry. But for stores, however familiar, there's never been a guarantee of people walking through their front door. All the ups and downs and maddening vicissitudes of business were in play from the beginning. Stores are not churches. It's not enough for regulars to simply show up. They have to buy stuff.

"The problem for country store owners is that they are not mythology," writes Dennis Bathory-Kitsz, author of *Country Stores of Vermont*. "They're the real thing, they need real customers, they have to be a real and vibrant part of the community."

In other words, in addition to often being longtime, local landmarks, general stores struggle constantly to remain relevant and stay solvent—and needed—in their communities. And the wider world beyond today doesn't make it easy.

"It's a constant challenge in the world of box stores and franchises, and we're up against that every day," cautions Jack Garvin, owner of the Warren Store in Warren, Vermont. "You have to be innovative all the time, have your ear to the ground and really listen to your customers and what they want."

Sometimes that still doesn't work. Garvin has a strategy for when your ideas as a store owner don't work out.

"'Fail fast and fail cheap,' I call it," he laughs. "If an idea doesn't get traction and take off, we move on to something else. If that one new idea didn't work out, there are fifteen to twenty other ideas behind it we'll roll out. Keep trying things."

And stores do. They have to. They try great coffee and good Wi-Fi, breakfast specials and extensive lunch menus. They try trendy beer and wine tastings, live music, local art, poetry readings, and cooking lessons. And they make sure there are choices of eggs, breads, cheese, and chips. Other stores have tried whole other directions, giving up the groceries all together. In Mansfield, Massachusetts, and Chepachet, Rhode Island, centuries-old stores still open for business every day, but the goods are different now than they were decades ago. This is okay. There is no one-size-fits-all for general stores. It's what works.

"Even with community support, they do need to be successful," says Paul Bruhn, executive director of the Preservation Trust of Vermont. "It's about finding niches where you can make a profit. You have to find what works in your community, which is different from somewhere else."

In establishing a niche, even a new and different one, existing stores may manage to survive, and the footprint they occupy is still linked to local history and tradition instead of a new business on the same footprint and linked to an anonymous central franchise office in Phoenix or Atlanta.

Because, ultimately, that's what general stores represent: something of, by, and for the local community. Those that survive and thrive have managed to keep the support of their community even when other choices exist. That is a triumph that goes beyond tasty food and a good craft beer selection. And that's especially true where a community has faced down the prospect of losing their store. In South Acworth, Harrisville, Barnard, and yes, Putney, that support is a triumph and a testament to the very notion and *need* for community itself. A need for that elusive but yearned-for "third place," where one can step out of the roles of work and home or the anonymity of the city and simply be among the familiar faces of . . . neighbors. In today's stressed society where things often feel more and more fractious and faceless, that need is stronger than ever and likely accounts for why it's possible to feel encouraged and optimistic about the survival of general stores as a cherished American institution. You can get a quart of milk anywhere; you can't get it with a smile and a "Hey, how's it going, Harold?" anywhere.

They knew that feeling for a long, long time in Bath, New Hampshire. There, the Brick Store, which was built over 200 years ago, thrived for centuries, and customers dropped in daily for their mail, not to mention the store's trademark fudge, buttermilk donuts, and smoked cheese. (In 2007, then-candidate Barack Obama dropped in with his daughters.) But in 2016, buffeted by a bad economy and some other local issues, the store—at the time considered possibly America's oldest, continuously operating general store—closed. The National Register of Historic Places was prepared to cross one place off its list, but someone said, "Not so fast." The store was sold at auction in July 2016, and locals Scott and Becky Mitchell bought it.

"My husband grew up here, I met him thirty-four years ago and I have been going to the Brick Store ever since," says Becky. "When they closed for the winter and then they didn't open, it just got sadder and sadder. We didn't want to see it go to something else, like condos or anything other than the Brick Store. It's really the heart of the town of Bath."

So the Mitchells have been doing some major surgery on that heart. We can report it's been revived; it's beating again. The store is spruced up and renovated and is expected to reopen in 2017. Who knows? In time, the Brick Store may once again become the nation's oldest, continuously operating general store.

Elsewhere, in other small towns around New England, there is also a renewed interest in saving or reviving general stores. Ask Robert DuGrenier, president of the nonprofit that saved the West Townshend Country Store.

"Other communities come to us and say, 'How did you do it?' and, 'What is your secret formula?' And really, it was just concerned people who didn't want to lose a tradition that we've had in America for hundreds of years—having that sense of community, a sense of help, a sense of need. And we just didn't want to lose that."

Who would? Let's not.

Acknowledgments

As with writing my first two books, I owe my greatest thanks and appreciation to my wife, Anne-Marie. A former journalist herself, she is the best pair of eyes I have, and hers are the first to read what I write. Her comments are unfailingly helpful. With this book, I had the added assistance of her direct involvement, even before a word was written—the idea for the book was hers. Her research and writing (not to mention her superior organizing) were invaluable, as were her good cheer, encouragement, and friendship. I am so grateful.

We owe enormous thanks, as well, to my friend and former colleague Art Donahue. An award-winning journalist and longtime photographer, Art is responsible for more than half the photos in this book. Few photographers have a better sense and feel of New England. Fewer still have his eye and his patience. Or fortitude. (He once produced a piece that involved shooting in all six New England states in a single calendar day.) Art covered a lot of ground for this book, driving sometimes before dawn to visit a lot of far-flung general stores. And at each stop, he did his usual wonderful work. We feel fortunate and honored for his role in this book.

We owe a special thanks to Paul Bruhn, executive director of the Preservation Trust of Vermont. Paul is as humble as he is helpful. Under his guidance, the PTV is doing extraordinary work, not only helping to empower communities and save more than buildings, but sometimes the soul of those communities themselves.

Thanks to Jack Garvin, owner of the Warren Store in Warren, Vermont, as well as to Robert Schroeder, president of the Robie's Country Store Historic Preservation Corporation.

At Globe Pequot, thank you to my editor, Amy Lyons, as well as the continued great work and unfailing help of Shana Capozza and Amy Alexander.

Thank you, once more, to Bryan Kelleher, from WCVB-TV, as well as my colleague Clint Conley, who shares the same love of small-town New England and its general stores.

And, of course, we are ultimately most indebted to all of the general store owners, past and present, who gave us their time and their thoughts, without which this book could not have been completed. And without whom New England would be missing so much. Thank you for keeping the lights on and putting the Open sign out every day. And for continuing to make that longed-for "third place" a reality for so many.

Appendix: General Stores by State

Connecticut

Colebrook Store, 25
559 Colebrook Road
Colebrook, CT 06021
(860) 379-5031
colebrookstore.net

Cornwall Country Market, 116
25 Kent Road S
Cornwall Bridge, CT 06754
(860) 619-8199
cornwallcountrymarket.com

Maine

Hussey's General Store, 132
510 Ridge Road
Windsor, ME 04363
(207) 445-2511
husseysgeneralstore.com

Sheepscot General at Uncas Farms, 163
98 Town House Road
Whitefield, ME 04353
(207) 549-5185
sheepscotgeneral.com

Massachusetts

The Brewster Store, 33
1935 Main Street
Brewster, MA 02631
(508) 896-3744
brewsterstore.com

Fern's, 111
8 Lowell Road
Carlisle, MA 01741
(978) 369-0200
fernscountrystore.com

Granville Country Store, 38
11 Granby Road
Granville, MA 01034
(413) 357-8555
granvillecheesestore.com

Harvard General Store, 125
1 Still River Road
Harvard, MA 01451
(978) 430-0062
harvardgeneralstore.com

Marshfield Hills General Store, 106
165 Prospect St
Marshfield, MA 02050
(781) 834-8443
marshfieldhillsgeneralstore.com

Monterey General Store, 169
448 Main Road
Monterey, MA 01245
(413) 528-5900
monterey-general-store.com

Wayside Country Store, 13
1015 Boston Post Road E #1
Marlborough, MA 01752
(508) 481-3458
waysidecountrystore.com

New Hampshire

Calef's, 53
606 Franklin Pierce Hwy
Barrington, NH 03825
(800) 462-2118
calefs.com

Harrisville General Store, 73
29 Church Street
Harrisville, NH 03450

(603) 827-3138
harrisvillegeneralstore.com

The Old Country Store & Museum, 5
1011 Whittier Highway
Moultonborough, NH 03254
(603) 476-5750
nhcountrystore.com

Robie's Country Store, 98
9 Riverside Street
Hooksett, NH 03106
(603) 485-7761
rootsatrobies.com

South Acworth Village Store, 60
1068 Route 123A
South Acworth, NH 03607
(603) 835-6547
acworthvillagestore.com

Rhode Island

Wilbur's General Store, 122
50 Commons
Little Compton, RI 02837
(401) 635-2356
wilbursgeneralstore.com

Vermont

Barnard General Store, 83
6231 VT-12
Barnard, VT 05031
(802) 234-9688
friendsofbgs.com

Dan & Whit's, 147
319 Main Street
Norwich, VT 05055
(802) 649-1602
danandwhitsonline.com

Jericho Center Country Store, 17
25 Jericho Center Circle
Jericho Center, VT 05465
(802) 899-3313
jerichocountrystore.com

Pittsfield Original General Store, 156
3963 Route 100
Pittsfield, VT 05762
(802) 746-8888
vermontsoriginalstore.com

Putney General Store, 90
4 Kimball Hill
Putney, VT 05346
(802) 387-4692
putneygeneralstore.com

Shrewsbury Co-op at Pierce's Store, 67
2658 Northam Road
Shrewsbury, VT 05738
(802) 429-3326
piercesstorevt.com

The Vermont Country Store, 140
657 Main Street
Weston, VT 05161
(802) 824-3184
vermontcountrystore.com

The Warren Store, 45
284 Main Street
Warren, VT 05674
(802) 496-3864
warrenstore.com

West Townshend Country Store, 179
6573 Route 30
West Townshend, VT 05359
(802) 874-4800
westtownshend.wixsite.com/wrcp

Index

About the Authors

Ted Reinstein has been a reporter for Chronicle, WCVB-TV/Boston's—and America's—longest-running locally produced nightly newsmagazine since 1997. In addition, he is a regular contributor to the station's weekly political roundtable show and sits on the station's editorial board. He is the author of *New England Notebook: One Reporter, Six States, Uncommon Stories* (Globe Pequot Press, 2013) and *Wicked Pissed: New England's Most Famous Feuds* (Globe Pequot Press, 2016). He lives just west of Boston with his wife and two daughters.

Anne-Marie Dorning is an Emmy Award–winning journalist and writer. She has covered presidential elections, breaking news stories around the nation, and the Olympic Games overseas. In addition to her work as a journalist, Anne-Marie, together with her husband, Ted, created their own communications company that serves a range of clients from local retail stores to Fortune 500 financial companies. This is her first collaboration on a full-length book. In her "spare" time, Anne-Marie works in communications at a New England college. She is also the mother of two amazing girls and lives west of Boston.